Music Is Medicine

Music Is Medicine

Dr. Miklós Pohl OAM

First published 2024

Copyright © Miklós Pohl OAM 2024
Copyright © on these stories remains with the individual writers
Copyright © on the photographs remains with the individual photographers

The moral rights of the author have been asserted.

All rights are reserved, except as permitted under the Australian Copyright Act 1968 (for example, fair dealing for the purposes of study, research, criticism or review). No part of this book may be reproduced, stored in a retrieval system, communicated or transmitted in any form or by any means without prior written permission from the author.

Every effort has been made to trace (and seek permission for the use of) the original source of material used within this book. Where the attempt has been unsuccessful, the publisher would be pleased to hear from the author or publisher to rectify any omission.

Cover design and typeset by BookPOD

ISBN: 978-1-7637683-0-7 (paperback) eISBN: 978-1-7637683-1-4 (ebook)

 A catalogue record for this book is available from the National Library of Australia

Profits from the sale of this book will be donated to

Please consider making a tax-deductable donation to MND Victoria:
www.mnd.org.au/music-is-medicine

Foreword

Covid's enforced musical desert has allowed me to put this book together, it was also my sanity and fun. I felt privileged to be allowed to enter my fellow Musical-Medicos lives, I know them much better now and feel closer to them even though I have played with some for 28 years. The fact is that when you play in a large orchestra such as ADO, you socialise very little. The intense 4-day schedule of rehearsals leading up to the concert on the Sunday leaves time for little else but playing. Those who don't play an instrument may not realise that learning, rehearsing and performing is hard work, both mental and physical. I enjoyed the honesty of everyone recounting their stories, their love of music and how everyone came to choose their instruments.

One of our more senior cellists (84), came up to me at our last concert and said; 'Miki this will be my last concert with ADO.'

'Why is that John? You are still playing so well.'

'It's not that, I can't physically handle the 8-hour rehearsals, I get too exhausted'

We were very sad to see him go as not only was he a good cellist he had also been with the orchestra since its inception in 1993.

The Australian Doctors Orchestra

ADO's last concert was in Orange in May 2020. A pandemic was declared the week of our concert, there were even rumours that a few Covid-19 cases had been detected in Orange but most of us didn't take any notice. I found it odd that a few colleagues, who were much better informed than I wouldn't shake hands but only offered their elbows in greeting.

There is a fountain in the open square of the Orange Performing Arts Centre, it was turned off, it looked like the Covid-19 virus, spikes emanating from a round ball. I asked a couple of friends to pose with me……. We thought it was a bit of a laugh at the time ……. Now it's not so funny. I wonder if the council will keep it now or commission something else to replace it!!

You can see why surgeons would make very bad actors!

A little about Covid-19

This RNA virus is made up of 30,000 base pairs. The human genome has 3 billion base pairs, it's humbling that something so 'insignificant' in size can grind the whole world to a halt and kill so many people.

The Orange concert was sold out and there were 500 people at the Sunday afternoon's performance.

One of the great pleasures of being in an orchestra is the joy of being inside a giant sound-making machine. Most professional musicians experience some hearing loss during their career. You may have noticed acoustic perspex shields in front of the brass section to reduce the sound reaching the woodwinds and the strings in front of them. ADO's founding conductor, Chris Martin, used to say that all professional musicians suffer some hearing loss, and then he added, 'but what a nice way to go deaf.'

Foreword

The Interviews

The interviews revealed some interesting trends. Everyone had a story about things that went wrong during a performance, so it's safe to assume that that is the norm. Two brief asides, the wonderfully talented composer-pianist Larry Sitsky played us his CD recording of Busoni's piano music at a Mt. Buller Chamber Music Camp for one year. The recording was note perfect, beautifully played, not a note out of place. At the end of the track he said, 'I wish I could play as well as that! 'All recordings are heavily edited till close to perfect.

The great Russian pianist / composer Sergei Rachmaninoff, on hearing one of his Ampico Player Piano Rolls said;

'Where are the mistakes?'

It must have sounded hilarious in a deep Russian voice and accent. Editing out the wrong notes would have entailed pasting over the holes in the piano rolls! Analog era at its best. They reassured him that people would not enjoy hearing the mistakes repeatedly.

Knowing that no performance is ever without a glitch will help us with future performances. This is clearly to be the NORM, not the exception!

The other emerging trend was that in most cases, it was our parents who encouraged us to start learning and persevere with our instruments. Things have shifted. Most schools now have large music programs, providing students with instruments as well as providing purpose built concert halls, which can often seat audiences of up to 400.

ADO beginnings

There are many Doctors Orchestras in the world, on every continent and too numerous to list. The earliest one I came across was founded in 1938. There are even Doctor's Orchestras made up of one specialty. There is an 'Ear, Nose and Throat Surgeons Orchestra in Italy.

Professor Ben Freedman (Violin) and Professor Michael Field (Flute), both contemporaries at the University of Sydney, devised a Music Medicine degree in 2006.

It all started at the Mount Buller Summer School for Strings (MBSSS) in 1993.

The Flow on Effect

Since its inception, numerous other doctors orchestras have sprung up throughout Australia, in every state and territory. There are also medical students orchestras in all states and territories.

ADO encourages both graduates and undergraduates, as well as all allied health professionals such as nurses and physios to join our happy band!

Doctoring is an exacting, demanding, and stressful profession. Music is a wonderful way to cope with these stresses. Some people play sport, others meditate or go to ashrams, and others still get an endorphin hit by playing music.

Foreword

Music Is Medicine

Foreword

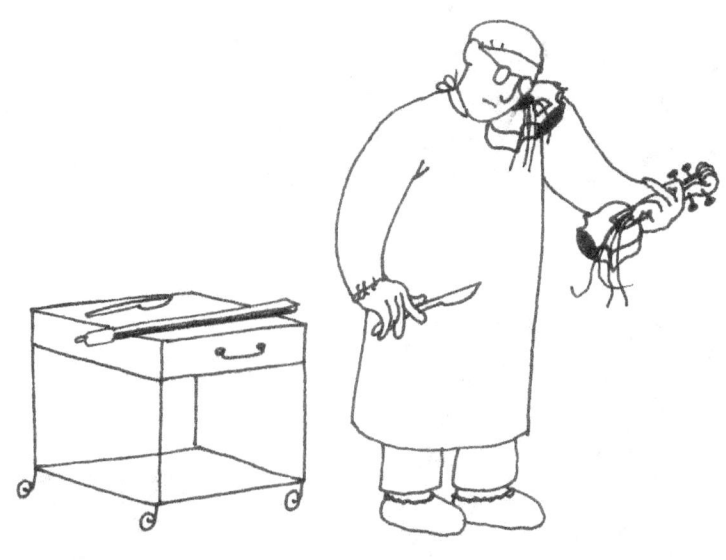

Contents

Introduction   1
My Fascination with Violins

Dr. Rowan Thomas   5
Anaesthetist, Violin, Founding Concert Master, ADO

Lindy Clarke   17
Pathologist, Cello

Annie Chen   22
Neurosurgical Trainee, ADO Treasurer, Violin

Barbara Manovel   27
General Practitioner, Cello

The Purpose of Music   30

Dr. Catherine Brennan   35
General Practitioner, Trumpet, Cello, Piano

Dr Peter Purches   49
General Practitioner, Violin, Trombonee, Arranger

Bronwyn Francis   54
Paediatrician, Violin, Viola

Phillip Antippa OAM   59
Cardio Thoracic Surgeon, Principal Founding Viola, ADO
Founder of Corpus Medicorum

Dr. Cathy Fraser   62
General Practitioner, Flute, Piccolo

The Violin As a Passport   68

Benjamin Martin   76
Concert Pianist, ADO Soloist

Dr Chris Hughes Obstetrician Gynaecologist, Double Bass	86
Dr Stuart Paige Anaesthetist, Bass Trombone	92
Jeffrey V. Rosenfeld AC, OBE, KStJ Emeritus Professor, Senior Neurosurgeon, Adjunct Professor in Surgery, Clinical Professor (Honorary), Adjunct Professor (Research), Professor (Honorary), Major General (Ret'd), Australian Defence Force, Clarinet	97
The Joy of the Amateur	111
Bridie Mee General Practitioner, Oboist	113
Osman Ozturk Anaesthetist, Violinist Past Concertmaster ADO	122
Dr. Anita Green General Practitioner, French Horn	129
Dr. Bonnie Fraser General Practitioner, Percussion	136
The Power of Music and Musical Raspberries	142
Dr Tony Prochazka Cosmetic Doctor, Cello	144
Miklós (Miki) Pohl OAM Plastic Surgeon, Violin, Viola, Founder of ADO	154
Dr Anna Glue General Practitioner, Cello, Current ADO President	161
Dr Jean McMullin General Practitioner, Violin, Viola, Trombone	169
Music As a Means of Social Change, 'El Sistema'	180

Sonia Baldock Critical Nurse Educator, Violin, ADO Concertmaster	184
Dr Janis Svilans Anaesthetist, Cellist	192
Rick McQueen-Thomson General Practitioner, Trumpet, Cello	200
Naham Warhaft Anaesthetist, Tuba	206
Dr Philip Griffin Plastic Surgeon, Viola	214
Dr. Rachel Lind Emergency Physician, Cello	221
Mary Frost Psychiatrist, Viola	228
Listen to This	238
ADO Past Presidents	246
Acknowledgements	247

Introduction

My Fascination with Violins

How many objects are 450 years old and in use every day at work? I can only think of one. The Violin……ok, ok, cellos, violas, and double bases as well of course but let's just stick to the violin.

There is something pleasing to the eye in the beautiful curves of a stringed instrument. Perhaps in the subconscious, it is the female form, certainly from a man's perspective. It's interesting that not all violins are feminine in character. Certainly, some are petite and have a femaleness about them, but others are masculine in character.

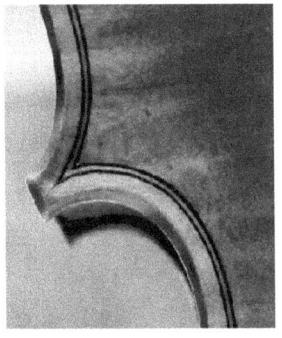

Each handmade instrument has its own personality and is unique. Amongst the more famous, Luthiers, Amati, Stradivarius, Guarneri, Guadagnini had their own ideas about design and form. The lengths of violins are fairly standard, but their shapes are quite different. Violas, Cellos and Double Basses have varying sizes and many different shapes. You will hear modern makers say things like, 'It's a Guarneri model'. What they mean is that they used Guarneri's templates for their modern creations. Newly made instruments

can rival old instruments in sound as shown in many double-blind listening trials.

I love holding old violins looking at their battle scars, scratches, dents, and chipped edges. The patina on an old violin speaks to me of its journey. Modern instrument makers ask their clients, 'Would you like your instruments antiqued?' Which means making the instrument look older than it is. They achieve this by denting, scratching, and beating the instruments ever so gently, to achieve the desired effect.

My viola was made in Chicago, by master maker Kiernoziak in 2006, it's a beautiful instrument both in appearance and sound, it has been gently antiqued, in very good taste, not overdone. My violin on the other hand is thought to be Italian, made around 1850, it has no label inside, and it has aged naturally over 170 years of use. Choosing one's instrument is an interesting process. There is magic, and romance involved, it's not dissimilar to falling in love.... I am serious. I remember when my violin arrived in Hobart from Melbourne in its heavy aluminium travel case. It sat there for 3 days before I had the time to open the case.

It was like being struck by a bolt of lightning. It was love at first sight and I knew I had found my instrument even before I put bow to string. It had a deep, rich, resonant, silky quality of sound, across all the strings.

Same thing happened when I asked Richard Tognetti[1] to try my 'new' violin. But this time it was my bow. I opened the case, he completely ignored my violin and homed straight

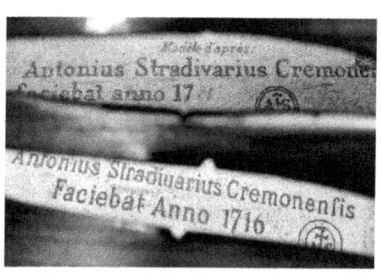

Strad labels, d'aprés above and the real thing below

---

1   Richard Tognetti is Leader of the internationally famous Australian Chamber Orchestra.

Introduction

in on my Voirin bow (French 1860s), he subsequently borrowed it to record the Haydn violin concertos. He left me his Sartori bow (also French) till he finished the recordings.

Should you ever visit the Ashmolean Museum in Oxford, go and see the 'Stradivarius' violin nicknamed 'The Messiah'. It is housed in a crystal, climate-controlled sarcophagus, the same as the one the Crown Jewels are held in , in the Tower of London. It earned its nickname because it has never been played, well hardly ever. Antonio hung on to it and never sold it. Then it came into the possession of the greatest of French instrument makers, Vuillaume. He couldn't part with it either. The point being that IT LOOKS BRAND NEW! No character-patina at all, its beauty is entirely in the shape, and the quality of craftsmanship by the greatest of all masters. Patina is desirable, it gives an instrument character.

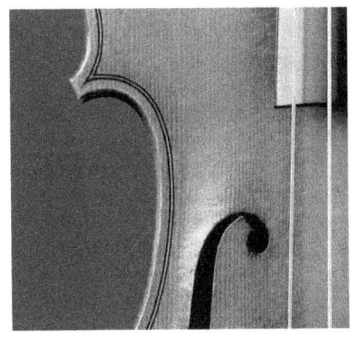

Note the exquisite detailing, there were no power tools in 1710.

The Messiah is taken out and played occasionally. Instruments need human contact; they dry up and are prone to woodworm without it. They also need to vibrate to keep healthy and well. I feel sorry for 'The Messiah', it's crying out to be held and played more.

Banks, wealthy individuals, and large corporations frequently buy valuable old instruments such as Tognetti's Guarneri valued at $10 million. It is rumored that Russell Crowe bought and loaned it to him after filming "Master and Commander".

Richard taught him to mime playing in the movie. Most of these extraordinary instruments are on loan to famous soloists who have the use of them for the duration of their performing careers, then they must either return them or pass them on to the next generation of players. As one old friend who owned a beautiful old cello said, 'We are merely custodians of these precious gifts.'

Dr. Rowan Thomas

MBBS, FANZCA,
MPH, Grad Dip Health Informatics

Anaesthetist, Violin
Founding Concert Master, ADO

'I love how string instruments go through your body and resonate within'

Miki

Seriously considering the idea of becoming a professional musician, Rowan studied intensively with Chris Martin, Spiros Rantos, and others in his teen age years. It is our good fortune that he chose medicine putting him in the perfect position to be the inaugural concert master of ADO.

I met Rowan at the 1993 Mt Buller Summer Camp for Strings. It was serendipity that both he and Chris Martin were there as I had been thinking of starting an Australian Doctors Orchestra for some time. Rowan was not only a beautiful violinist, but he also had other qualities that make for a great Concert Master. He has a calm, encouraging manner, spoke confidently with authority, suggesting bowings, fingerings and how to shape (phrase) the music. He is affable and approachable, all of which makes for an ideal leader. Personally, I have learnt more about violin playing from him than anyone else over our 30 years friendship.

What does music mean to you in your life?

It's a way of getting away from the materialistic rat race of having to earn money and get ahead and do more and more. Music is meditative, solid, and more enjoyable. I love the resonance of the string instruments, the way they go through your body and resonate within you. That contact and the fact that you can combine with people whom you wouldn't normally even strike up a conversation and still share a moment. There is something about synchronicity that is important for us. If you can share in a moment, and make the same mistake, do something, and understand exactly what that person is thinking, then that's one of the closest things that you can share with another person.

What was your earliest musical recollection?

My earliest musical recollections were the sounds that go with advertisements on the radio. We got a TV when I was about 10 years old, there were musical jingles and entertainment of other sorts. That was my total experience of what music was. My father had an old record player, rarely played, but he had four or five LPs one of which was Rossini's 'The Thieving Magpie'. I listened to that one day and was astounded that music could be so directed, complex and engaging for its own sake. I was about nine or ten and I got my own little radio and would fall asleep listening to it.

I decided to learn the guitar because most of the songs on the radio involved the guitar. I learned from a gentleman called Sergio and was very frustrated because when I played it didn't sound terrific straight away. 'Well, that's because you have to work on it, you have to practise.' We'd have arguments with me saying, 'but I want to play now.' I spent two long years with him trying to teach me how to practise so that I could actually play something better. I learnt some chords and some Flamenco, and I sang a bit with the guitar, but I gave up lessons after two years because I really didn't like practising.

I was in the church choir; the choir master was also a piano teacher. He said that in order to understand music better, you could probably see all of the notes on the piano keys, that kind of made sense. So, I learnt the piano with him to about grade five. I would have probably been 14 or 15 when I stopped learning from him.

So how did you end up being such a great violinist?

(Rowan laughs at that comment.)

I was in second form (year 8) at school and each of the music teachers would come around and they would get you to try out an instrument.

The first one was a trumpet. We all had a blow, and I scored a B for my sound on the trumpet, having never been taught anything about embouchure or anything like that. So, I was told to learn the trumpet. Then the next week a violin teacher at Scotch College brought around some violins. The night before, I visited the piano teacher's son called Christopher who was learning the violin. Christopher had chores to do so I asked if I could look at his violin and a book of the first 30 lessons. I used what I'd learned through piano and guitar to work out what the fingering on the violin would be, and just sort of taught myself how to hold the instrument and make a sound.

How old were you then?

Probably about 15. I taught myself how to play 'Twinkle Twinkle Little Star'. The next day, the teacher brought out 20 violins and gave them to the class and said, 'I'll show you how to play 'Twinkle Twinkle Little Star' once, then I want you to see how far you can get through it. Then he showed us how to play it, what the notes were and where the fingers had to go.

I plucked 'Twinkle Twinkle Little Star' from beginning to end. He said, 'Have you played the violin before?'

'No'

'You're coming with me right now. Here is the book of Muller-Rush, first 30 lessons. I want you to learn those for next week.'

I went home and learnt the first 30 lessons and then I was chastised the following lesson because I wasn't at Orchestra.

'What Orchestra?'

'Your name was on the list, and you didn't turn up.'

So, I joined the school orchestra in the second week, and we were playing Berlioz's Symphony Fantastique'. Having learned violin for one week, the noise I made was horrendous, but it didn't matter, there were one hundred kids playing trombones, clarinets, and other string instruments. Whatever you did with your fingers, you couldn't hear yourself let alone anything else. That piece required playing in all positions[2], so I needed the second book to teach me how to do that.

You hadn't had a formal lesson at all until this point?

No, I was thrown in at the deep end, then having to play in all sorts of different positions. My teacher said, 'if you play the violin, you'll never ever make it because violinists are a dime a dozen. They're all very competitive and high achievers. If you really want to make it in the musical world, learn the viola, the viola has a beautiful sound. It is very lush.'

After week three, I converted to the viola in the orchestra, which uses a completely different clef to the violin, and I had never seen alto clef before in my life. Scotch College had a big orchestra, there were a hundred people in the main orchestra. All of them had been cajoled, enlisted, or bullied into playing. George Logie-Smith used to go around the classes saying "Jones, why aren't you learning a musical instrument?"

---

2   Positions means moving up the fingerboard from basic first to 7,8 or higher up the fingerboard, the higher the more difficult.

When he got to me, he said, "Thomas, why aren't you learning two musical instruments?"

My violin teacher's teaching method was not one I'd seen before or since then. Basically, it involved telling me that every note was either flat or sharp, so I would play the note and he'd say 'flat', I wasn't quite sure what that meant.

I would play the next note 'You're sharp', I wasn't sure if that was a compliment or not, but if I had any sense of pitch, it was very quickly destroyed over the next three months. When I played on my own, it sounded disgusting. In orchestra you couldn't hear yourself, so it was fine. At the end of that year, my parents gave me a viola for Christmas.

How old were you then?

I would have been 16 and I burst into tears.

'Don't get me a viola, I hate the instrument, it's the devil's work, it's horrible.'

Rowans Father 'But we thought you liked it.'

Rowan 'Well, yeah, in orchestra, but on its own, it's revolting. There's no way I'll play it long term.' Rowans Father 'Tell us about the lessons and tell us about your teacher?

I described a lesson, and they thought, well, maybe a different teacher might help.

The trouble is that if I learned from a different teacher at the school, it would have been embarrassing
confronting my current teacher.

'You don't have to learn from the teacher at school'.

'But I like the orchestra and you have to learn from the schoolteachers in order to stay in the orchestra.'

'Okay. What if you had extra lessons?'

They found Barbara Argall and when she heard me play, she said:

'Ah, this is terrible we've got to go back to step one, preliminary; this is how you put your fingers on the fingerboard and this is how you move the bow, and this is the sound you have to make.'

We went right back to the beginning; she worked in a way that I could understand and enjoy. She organised smaller groups called 'Sunday morning breakfast Bach to Bacharach'.

She was very enthusiastic, and you'd hear other students whilst you were waiting because she always ran late. Other people would hear your playing, all in all it was a lovely environment. I wanted to work really, really hard for her and by the time I was in year 12 I played with the Victorian Junior Symphony Orchestra and the Victorian Concert Orchestra which toured the state. I also played with the Kelmier Orchestra, which later became Aussie Pops. I also really enjoyed all the social aspects music had to offer, that was my passport to fun and socialising.

I started formal lessons when I was 16, then by the time I was 18 I was doing sixth and seventh grade pieces. Well enough for HSC and the result was included in my top four for the high school certificate, VCE equivalent now. Once at university we started a small chamber orchestra at Monash. Yes, and it's been through its ups and downs. Bronwyn Francis played in it and a few others who I still see, I conducted whenever we needed a conductor. The orchestra had a disproportionate number of medicos.

When I started to play L. Mus level pieces Barbara Argall sent me to learn from Chris Martin for a year. At every lesson he'd say, 'Ah, what else have you got in your bag that I haven't heard you play?' He'd go through that piece and say, 'Yeah, yeah, we'll do something else next week.' By the end of the year we had played through the entire viola repertoire. There was nothing left to play.

I thought, maybe I should change to the violin, I was 20 then and decided to take a year off from Medicine. I was wondering if medicine was really the thing I wanted to do.

I auditioned for Beryl Kimber in Adelaide and Spiros Rantos in Toowoomba. Spiros was very keen to have me, and I enjoyed practising on average eight hours a day for Spiros. There were only three major violin students with him at the time, as it was a recently established music course. He would spend as many hours as I could spare. We would have three-hour lessons, go through scales, studies, and pieces. There were only two days that year that I didn't practice. The most I would practise was 10 hours a day, but on average about eight. I got most of my 10,000 hours with Spiros, on the violin in Toowoomba between my third and fourth year of Medical School.

How did he end up in Melbourne founding the Rantos Academy?

He stayed in Chris Martin's house when he was overseas on sabbatical. He took over all of Chris's students. On Chris's return and after changing to the violin, I went back to Chris to give me some pointers on how to play some violin pieces.'

I had been playing the violin for a month, learning, 'Ziguenerweisen' as well as Mendelssohn's violin concerto.

I played the Mendelssohn violin concerto for Chris and at the end of the first movement he stopped me.

'You know, I've probably heard this played more than a thousand times by as many people and to this day, I have never ever heard it played well. You should put it away and take it up again when you're 40.'

Well, he was right about that. The actual technical parts of it were not too difficult, but the music is very challenging.

What were your most exciting musical experiences, as a player and as a listener?

I've had more exciting musical experiences as a player. Music camp, playing in the first violin section of the second orchestra, I also led the second orchestra one year. To have every player play exactly the same rhythm and the same pitch is a brilliant experience in a violin section. I also played in Australian Youth Orchestra as a Violist.

As a listener there were many exciting moments, but generally, I prefer to be a participant rather than a listener.

Did you ever have a musical ahaha moment?

Listening to the Beaux Art Trio when we were in Ithaca, upstate New York, at Cornell University, it was 1997 and I was disappointed. They played like a recording and didn't put any effort or energy into it. I had befriended the senior lecturer in strings at Cornell and I commented to her afterwards that I was surprised that I wasn't as moved as I should have been.

'Yes, absolutely.'

'They think they can come to Ithaca and think that they're playing in some hick town, but they've got to give us a New York City performance. You know, we're discerning musicians. I was as disappointed as you.'

She was furious and was going to go backstage to give them a piece of her mind.

It was a genuine response, they probably did have times when they turned it on in the bigger towns, but it didn't feel like it then.

A positive ahaha moment was when Pinchas Zuckermann and Itzhak Perlman played Mozart's 'Sinfonia Concertante' at Carnegie Hall in New York in 1997. We got the worst seats in the hall for $300 each. It was some sort of charity concert; it was with the Israel Philharmonic Orchestra. It's not always superb music or perfect music that moves you, it's the amount of effort and soul in the playing. Another moment was Maria Lurighi singing Villa-Lobos's 'Bachianas Brasileiras' at a Mt Buller Summer Music Camp, her singing transported me.

Music is different from communication, it's more about being in sync. It's about knowing that your time is moving at exactly at the same time as somebody else's. It's even more important now a days, because we all are growing up with a different experience because we can do things online. We can learn what we want to learn. It's not like everybody's watching the same TV program at night, like we used to and then be able to talk about it at work the next day. Every conversation you have, is about someone trying to introduce you to something that they've seen that you may not have seen, rather than saying, 'Oh wasn't it funny last night when so-and-so did such and such, it wasn't that great.' I think that's why art is also better when it's shared, people can look at the same piece of work and be in sync and say, 'Yes, that's it' and share that moment and those thoughts.

Can you remember when things went wrong in a performance?

The worst ones are so bad that they are funny. In my intern year I was playing at the Latrobe Valley Hospital Charity Concert. There was a general surgeon who played the piano. I was playing Csárdás by Monti and he was the accompanist. We had rehearsed it thoroughly. Sometimes he went into a bit of a dream while playing and at one stage he turned two pages at once and of course it just didn't work. I knew exactly what he'd done, and we stopped, I turned the page back for him and we started that section again.

What's your desert Island discs choices?

That's really hard because I'm hopeless at creating playlists that I know I'll enjoy listening to over and over.

I always like something new, so I end up having the radio on, even with the ads at least there is always something new playing.

I like the Mozart piano concertos and Beethoven's late string quartets but, as you know, they're all dead white guys, and there are things that I want to do that I haven't done yet like, listen to everything that Vaughan Williams wrote.

What about when we played his (RVW's) string quintet?

Yes, we got a little bit closer the other night, I've I played one of his symphonies and then there is The Lark Ascending and many other things that people know well.

What about Bach?

If I only had one piece of sheet music to play, then it would be the Bach Solo Violin Sonatas, I know from experience that I can spend hundreds of hours on just one of those.

Is there anything you would like to say about ADO?

The first Doctors Orchestra was after my first Mt. Buller Summer Camp at which I was going to be playing second violin in a quartet with Daniel Stefansky. He unfortunately got appendicitis, and suddenly I was promoted to first violin. Jason Bunn was originally the violist and moved to second violin, the cellist was Sven Eriksen. Sylvia Blatt from Sydney played viola, she was a last-minute ring-in and a good violist.

I had no idea what the standard was going to be. We decided to get together that afternoon to run through something that might be playable. We played through a Mendelssohn quartet, and we were committed to playing in the first cocktail hour. I was practising it furiously having just been thrown into the first violin position. We were a new quartet and had never played in front of a room full of strangers.

There was this crazy Hungarian guy who kept watching my fingers. He sat about a metre away from my violin and I was thinking, 'Oh, this would be terrible for him.' 'Why is he sitting so close?' He can probably tell every nuance of everything I'm doing wrong. I was terribly self-conscious, but we got through it. Then you came up straight afterwards and said, 'I'm going to start a doctors orchestra, I want you to lead it.' I thought, 'oh, he didn't think I was that bad after all.'

Where does ADO fit into your life?

While I was doing my anaesthetics training I didn't play at all for five years. Then I started playing with the Collingwood Chamber Orchestra. We played a gig at which my sister Meredith led. I was playing second violin and after the first piece she leant over and said, 'What has happened to your sound, it's disgusting?'

Spiros happened to be in Melbourne at the time and I got a lesson from him. He got me to do Kreutzer Study No 2 as loud and as powerfully strong as you can possibly play. He said he wanted every single note to crack because he reckoned that my right arm had become so weak from not having played for five years, that I couldn't produce a reasonable sound. A week of that got me back to playing.

Over a 12-year period The Australian Doctors Orchestra went from strength to strength and my involvement had been trying to be as good a concertmaster as I could be. Linking the conductor with the players. A particularly critical moment for me was to work out when it was time for me to move on. When I recognised players sitting behind me who were stronger players, I knew then that I could confidently hand over.

It's all about being a team.

I was listening to a podcast on leadership. The best leaders are those who will look at the people they're leading and be their biggest fans, no matter what they're doing. Whether they're doing really well or doing really badly, the leader has to be encouraging and rooting for them, saying, 'I know you can do it. You're the best there is.'

Lindy Clarke
Pathologist, Cello

'I couldn't imagine my life without music, it would be empty'

What was your earliest musical recollection?

My earliest musical recollection is at Ringwood Methodist Church. Hymn singing was lusty and a major part of the service, and my mother sang in the choir.

I was three. My mother had been a good pianist as a teenager and young woman, but I didn't hear her play until we got a piano when I was 11.

Did you have exposure to music when you were young?

Not really, apart from on the radio and at church. I always wanted to play the piano as a child. My best friend at primary school was learning the piano and I was so envious. I started learning piano at the age of eleven when I went to secondary school. I learnt the notes on a toy grand piano with painted black keys before my parents scraped together enough money to buy a piano. I started cello in form three (year 9) when I was 14.

My parents hired a school cello for me. I was already involved in music, singing in the choir and madrigal group, and then joined the school orchestra and string quartet. At the end of high school, I had to make a career decision: would I do music (like many of my friends) or medicine? I loved music and wasn't too bad at it, but I definitely made the right decision when I chose medicine.

Did you join an orchestra after that?

I was doing heaps of music when I was at secondary school. I also played in the Junior Symphony Orchestra (JSO), conducted by Stuart Wilkie. We rehearsed on Saturday mornings at the Melbourne Con.

I've played in various orchestras all my life and I've done lots of pit playing for musical theatre. I could probably play the cello part of "The Pirates of Penzance" from memory. I played with Whitehorse Musical Theatre, conducted by Doug Cliff. I particularly remember doing "West Side Story" with them - it was just fantastic.

In later years before moving to Brisbane I played in the Collingwood Chamber Orchestra.

I continued with my cello teacher, Peers Coetmore, and did my A.Mus.A when I was in fourth year Med. Peers was a graduate of the Royal College of Music and she'd been previously married to the English composer E. J. Moeran who wrote a cello concerto for her. She did a number of recital tours in Asia with the pianist Max Cooke: she was a fantastic teacher, although initially I was scared of her. She was somewhat eccentric. In winter she often wore a kilt, which she would wear back-to-front, because if you're a cellist you need all the fullness in the front. After I went to Uni, my lesson came last on Saturday mornings and we used to talk afterwards, my lessons could last two hours.

Those pivotal people are so important in our lives

Absolutely. There was another pivotal person in my life: my science teacher, Richard Keuneman's grandmother. She taught me maths and science in Form 3 (year 9) and that really awakened my interest in science. She was not only a very good teacher, but also a very good pianist, she showed me that you could do both. Later she accompanied me for my A.Mus.A. exam.

I graduated from Melbourne Uni in 1974 and did my residency at the Royal Melbourne Hospital. I was then invited to go back to Uni to do a PhD in pathology. As you know, pathology is the basis of all of medicine, so I decided to accept the opportunity and I completed my PhD in experimental glomerulonephritis. I was also doing autopsies at the Royal Melbourne and teaching pathology to undergraduates. At the end of my three-year PhD I was given two years credit by the College of Pathologists towards my five years of training.

It meant, however, that I came out a bit under-done: in Pathology we say that that you need "optical mileage" (hours at the microscope looking at slides), and my experience was a bit limited due to truncated years as a Path registrar. I coped because I have a photographic sort of mind. This also helps me with my cello playing because I visualise the positions on the fingerboard.

Did you manage to keep playing while you were having your babies?

I was still playing with Whitehorse and with Babirra Players. Our conductor at Babirra was openly gay and flamboyant - he used to turn up to concerts in an evening cloak with blue satin lining. The first thing I did on arriving in Brisbane in 1992 was to find an orchestra. I joined Brisbane Sinfonia, now the Brisbane Symphony Orchestra. I have played with them for nearly 30 years and now I'm the secretary of the organisation.

I also love playing chamber music with friends.

What was your most exciting experience as a player and as a listener?

As a listener there have been many, but probably the standout was hearing Jacqueline du Pré playing the Elgar concerto with MSO at the Melbourne Town Hall.

As a performer I remember the excitement of singing the Verdi Requiem with the MSO and the Melbourne Chorale, conducted by Hiroyuki Iwaki.

I also remember playing Mahler 1 with Brisbane Sinfonia shortly after relocating to Brisbane. I remember the sense of exhilaration when we got to the end of the last movement. I felt, "Wow, we've really done it": that was fantastic.

I've had so many highlights it's hard to pick out one or two.

What does music mean to you?

It's very much part of me; it's part of my life. I don't think I could live without it. It's a challenge. It keeps you alive intellectually and it moves you; it's an emotional experience. I could never imagine my life not having music to listen to or to play; it would be empty.

Can you remember a time when things went wrong in the performance?

Heaps of times. We had one chamber performance when we had to stop and start again. It was at a party for our 30th wedding anniversary, and we were playing a Brahms sextet. We got in a muddle, stopped and I said, "Let's go back". Nobody minded. As you know, we've had some hairy moments with ADO.

What would be your desert island choices?

In fact, I am trying to do that at the moment. I've been doing a series of recordings for 4MBS once a month, presenting works that the BSO has recorded. Last time the producer who looks after me asked me to do a desert island discs type program entitled "My journey in music". I'm struggling because the program is for an hour with only 35 minutes of music. I've decided on a movement from a Bach solo Cello Suite with YoYo Ma, and some of the Elgar with Jacqueline du Pré. What else? The Romantic era is my favourite, but the Bach Cello suites are unbelievable. I love the Dvorak and Elgar Cello Concerti, any of the Tchaikovsky Symphonies, Dvorak's symphonies (the 8th especially), Brahms symphonies and chamber music, the Beethoven String Quartets… It's very hard to choose.

How much do you practise?

Not enough is the answer. There are some weeks that I don't touch the cello and then I arrive at rehearsal and wish I had. Then there are other weeks when I'll practise for an hour or more on four or five consecutive days.

Annie Chen

Neurosurgical Trainee
ADO Treasurer, Violin

'Music is how I've met different people I connect with, it's a way of life'

Annie represents the young generation of ADO players. She is an accomplished violinist attesting to the opportunities afforded young musicians both at school and state level. Annie is currently ADO's treasurer; she executes this task efficiently and with great enthusiasm. Cheery of disposition, she is a 'can do' person and a tremendous asset to our orchestra.

How long have you been playing with ADO?

My first concert with ADO was in 2011, in Sydney.

What are your earliest musical recollections?

When I was 3 or 4 and we were still living in China, my Mum tried to introduce me to the violin but apparently after only a few lessons the teacher refused to continue teaching me as I was so inattentive and preferred to play with the teacher's children instead. A few years later, after moving to New Zealand, I began to learn the violin in earnest, but managed early on to hinder any progress by breaking my arm in the playground. Fortunately, I have been able to keep my limbs intact since and focus, most of the time, on playing the violin.

It was my Mum who loved classical music and the violin in particular. She did not herself play the instrument but instilled in me a deep appreciation for music and encouraged me to play. Between my violin lessons Mum would sit through my daily practice, demonstrating an extraordinary amount of patience.

When we arrived in Melbourne in 2001, I began studying with Mr. Lin Xiang, an absolutely kind and wonderful teacher who was a significant force in my musical development. Mr. Xiang was always generous with his praise, gentle with his criticisms and passionate about whatever he was teaching me at the time. He introduced me to a wide repertoire, encouraged me through my doubts and uncertainties and helped me attain my A. Mus.A and L.Mus. A.

Mr Xiang also managed a music store and found a violin for me that I still play today. Embarrassingly I don't actually recall much regarding the details about my violin, but it's been with me through all my various practices, exams and performances over the last 20 or so years and I don't think I could ever part with it. I have managed to knock a tiny corner off it after one particularly aggressive pizzicato, so I'm sure no one else would want it anyway.

From age 16, I played in the Melbourne Youth Orchestra (MYO) and had the privilege of being Concertmaster in 2008 and 2009. I joined Corpus Medicorum in my first year of medical school and
at university, also played with the Monash Academy Orchestra and the Monash Medical Orchestra, I was part of the founding committee.

My first concert with ADO was in 2011 but in all honesty, I can't remember how I was introduced to it! I think I've been part of ADO for so long that it's just become a regular part of my life.

Can you remember where music spoke to you?

My love of music stemmed from my Mum who played classical music to me at every opportunity. I'll hear a piece every now and then which will take me back to memories with my Mum of weekend breakfasts and long car drives. There are various moments both in playing solo pieces and in an ensemble setting where the music is overwhelming, and I find myself feeling astonished and so lucky to be able to be a part of creating and performing music as well as the ability to appreciate it. There's nothing quite like being part of a ensemble and working together in sync to bring written notes on a page to life.

What made you take up your instrument?

I think my Mum always wanted but was never able to learn an instrument herself, so she wanted to ensure I had that opportunity to learn the violin. I've since learned other instruments but have always come back to the violin.

What was your most exciting musical experience as a player and then as a listener?

As a player, one of the most memorable performances was my final concert with MYO as concert master. We opened at the Myer Music Bowl for an MSO concert and played Rachmaninov's 'Symphonic Dances' which is one of my favourite pieces. It was a beautiful day with a great atmosphere, and it just had that magic quality about it.

I played Introduction and Rondo Capriccioso by Saint-Saëns as the soloist with the Monash Medical Orchestra. That was memorable because I had wanted to play it for a very long time and now, I had the opportunity, with my family and friends in the audience and I had worked hard on learning it as best I could whilst studying medicine.

As a listener there are two performances that are truly memorable. I was in my final year Medicine, and I had the opportunity to do my elective term in England while the BBC Proms were on. Nigel Kennedy was playing 'Vivaldi's Four Seasons'. My friends and I didn't have tickets, so we lined up outside in the last minute tickets queue. We were amongst the last 10 or so people to get in and the performance, as you'd expect, was phenomenal. It was a pretty special experience.

I also had the chance to see Yo-Yo Ma in Melbourne perform all of the Bach Solo Cello Suites in one sitting. It was a mesmerising two and a half hours of continuous playing.

What does music mean to you?

You mentioned that the other day and I thought, how am I going to answer that? I think music has meant different things to me at different times of my life and it's a dynamic and evolving relationship. It's been such a fundamental part of my life growing up that I couldn't imagine life without music. I can't imagine not listening or thinking of my violin or when the next concert will be, or do I need a new black dress for the next performance. It's everywhere, it's linked to my relationship with my mother, it's how I've met different people I connect with on a day-to-day basis. It's a way of life.

It's also a way to connect and communicate with people, and now being older, I remember a time when I was a teenager, and I didn't want to practise but my Mum was very insistent that practised every day. It turned at one point into a yes, thinking, I have the skills to play and to be able express my emotions through my instrument, I have the opportunity to sit in an orchestra or a quartet, or play by myself and communicate all this.

Can you remember a time when things went wrong in a concert?

I'm quite a clumsy person, and I can recall on at least three occasions when I fell over going on or coming off stage. They are always memorable because you to try to look professional and keep your composure while at the same time you feel terribly embarrassed inside. I also played the bongos in a jazz dance piece at high school. It's the sort of thing you hope never happens to you, but I finished a beat late somehow and it was a very loud extra beat after everyone had finished playing. There was no hiding it!

What are your desert island choices?

I love Rachmaninov's Symphonic Dances and his First Piano Concerto. I would also take Khachaturian's violin concerto. My third choice is Dvorak, especially the Symphony no.9 ,'From the New World'. Every time I listen to it, I find something different in it.

Would you say your Mum was the most significant person in your musical life?

Absolutely. I can't thank my Mum enough for not only introducing me to music and violin, but also making certain I continued playing even when I wasn't as interested or when I was distracted.

What do you think about ADO?

What I love about larger ensemble music making is how many different people you meet. Even though we're a doctors orchestra, the same profession, it's still a diverse group of people. I love going to different states and cities to perform, pre-COVID, that is.

There's a real camaraderie that exists both within the orchestra and outside it, which coalesces and makes us play better together as a group. It also allows us to form new connections outside of music.

Barbara Manovel

MBBS, FRACGP

General Practitioner, Cello

'Music is an abiding passion; I cannot remember a time when it hasn't been a part of my life. Music adds spice, salt to life and it connects me in a deeply meaningful way to other people.'

Miki

You could sum up Barbara's personality as oozing 'Spanish effervescence.' Her playing is the same, she is a very fine cellist.

Both her parents are Spanish born and she arrived in Australia as a child. We are often reminded of her fluency in Spanish when she corrects our poor pronunciation of words like Manchego and Chorizo!

Barbara can't remember a time in her life when there wasn't any music. Although they didn't play an instrument as such, her parents loved classical music. Her first recollection of music was at the age of five when she saw Walt Disney's 'Fantasia'. The soundtrack was "The Sorcerer's Apprentice" by Dukas. The conductor, was the world-renowned Leopold Stokovsky with Mickey Mouse as the apprentice.

She recalls her parents' record player continually playing violin and piano concertos as she was growing up as well as Zarzuela….Spanish operetta.

My parents bought a piano and there followed a great love of piano music.

I learned the piano throughout school, then had to choose between Music and Medicine as many of us in ADO have. I think at some point in my early life, I realised that I wasn't born to be a performer.

I picked up the cello late in high school. My brother was a violinist and played in the school orchestra and it looked like a lot of fun. The piano is a very lonely instrument, but I continue to love piano music and find that it is very self-sufficient.

I was a very keen music student, but picked up the cello too late, and when I finished school, I did not play it much thereafter. When I finished Medicine, I worked, married and had three children; and all through that time I played the piano occasionally, for pleasure, and to accompany my son at his clarinet exams.

When I was pregnant with my youngest child, a friend of mine - John Gruner, who is a GP violinist, told me about ADO. He wanted to play chamber music and encouraged me to play cello with his group, so I picked up the cello again and started playing.'

My first ADO concert was in 2005 in Canberra with Max McBride conducting. I absolutely loved it, but also thought, 'Oh my goodness, I've got a long way to go.' I started having cello lessons again. With three children, a clinic and a farm, I didn't have much time but what I could find, I devoted to it.

I love playing in an orchestra; the result is more than the sum of its parts.

Joining ADO and meeting other doctors who were music tragics like me, who felt similarly passionate about music was very fulfilling.

Recalling the Sydney 2008 ADO concert:

I walked down into the hotel foyer and there was a quartet playing, Bronwyn Francis violin, Phillip Antippa viola, Janis Svilans cello, and Jean McMullin violin. I was entranced. I had not played much chamber music. As I listened to them, Janis offered me his cello, to have a go.

The sense that I could be a part of this sort of music-making was a revelation. After that I started playing in Corpus Medicorum and I also started playing in a quartet with Jean and Bronwyn (and Mary).

Barbara cites her most memorable musical experiences as a cellist, in Mahler's 4th. Symphony. As a listener, Stephen Hough's recital playing Beethoven, Chopin, and Scriabin. Her passion for piano music remains undiminished. She remembers one other very memorable musical moment which was at my house during one of my "Musical Kaffee Klatsch" gatherings. I put on a DVD of Hélène Grimaud playing the slow movement Ravel's Piano Concerto. 'Spine tingling!'

The Purpose of Music

What is the purpose of music? Does it have any purpose? Even people with a terrible ear who can't sing in tune seem to like it. I can't explain that. There is something deep in our genes that shows a desire for creating and listening to music.

We were giving a concert in Ljubljana with the European Doctors Orchestra in 2015. We had the honour of performing in the Philharmonie, a hall built in 1701 on the banks of the Lubljancina River.

The Philharmonie

Gustav Mahler

Behind the hall backing onto the river was a wonderful contemporary sculpture of Mahler. He was the resident conductor of the Ljubljiana Symphony in 1881.

Even more interestingly, in the caves above the city they found a flute now called the 'Divje Babe Flute' made of the long bone of a bear. Its holes have been trephined with the same spacing as a modern flute, allowing the production of different notes.

It's estimated to be 45,000 years old, the Neanderthal period. Cavemen were already making music then; this rudimentary flute is thought to be the oldest instrument in the world.

Music is communication, there is a wonderful YouTube recording of a man in Africa playing Beethoven's Moonlight sonata to an 80 year old blind bull elephant. The elephant stands next to the piano swaying gently to the music, he is clearly enjoying it and is comforted by it, the scene is very moving (Link below)

Music is Communication/https://youtu.be/4AcjvsVn5k

Music Is Medicine

I am often asked why so many doctors are musical and play an instrument. I don't think there is any mystery here. A lot of medicos come from middle to upper class backgrounds, they attended good schools where music was encouraged, and instruments and opportunity provided.

This was NOT the situation in my case, but I was lucky enough to be surrounded by classical music day and night at both my parents and my Aunt and Uncle's homes from early childhood.

There is another factor operating, Music is a form of communication and doctors like to communicate, not only with their patients but with colleagues in general.

Deutscher Grammophon tried to produce the "perfect" recording by putting each member of the Berlin Philharmonic Orchestra in their own recording cubicle. The cubicles were all miked separately. Can you imagine, a recording engineers' nightmare. Suffice it to say that the musicians could not play properly because they had lost communication with each other, so the whole project was scrapped.

There are many interesting papers written on music and the brain. It's not uncommon to be able reach people in nursing homes who have lost speech but still seem to be able to sing a tune when they hear something familiar. Music stimulates large areas of the brain. First, and most obviously the auditory centre, but it also stimulates the visual and motor cortices, as well as the frontal lobes which are responsible for higher reasoning and thought. The actual physicality of playing is often ignored. The sheer act of playing music lights up the whole brain. Playing for 2 to 4 hours is exhausting, both physically and mentally. Ask any professional or amateur. Even though it looks effortless, drawing a bow across the string requires remarkable muscular co-ordination and stamina.

All the principles of physics are invoked, pressure on the strings, the speed of the bow and friction between horsehair and string. The part of the string you are playing on also affects the sound, close to the bridge gives a glassy harsh sound which composers use to good effect. The technique is called 'ponti', (near the bridge). Playing over the fingerboard away from the bridge creates a soft ethereal sound, 'tasto'.

Dynamics, intonation and rhythm have to be observed. Musicality is an indefinable, unquantifiable gift that can't be learnt, you either have it or you don't.

In string class, we are asked to execute 'the one-minute bow'. You bow an open string for as long as you can, and at the same time you have to make a decent sound. Draw the bow too fast and you finish well under a minute, draw the bow slowly and no sound is produced at all or it's scratchy, not dissimilar to pulling out a rusty nail, too much pressure and it sounds like a tree stump being dislodged. Naturally you have to be 'in the zone' and very relaxed. I was usually the one to draw the longest bow till a snotty youth beat me. When I had finished there was still someone playing, Grrrrrrr, I was quite put out.

Jessye Norman, fabulous diva and an extraordinary Mezzo Soprano came to Sydney to sing Mahler's Kindertotenlieder (song for dead children) which he wrote just after he lost his beloved daughter, aged 3. Jessye was an enormous black woman, she was wearing what could best be describes as a 3 man tent!

As soon as she began to sing, three and a half thousand people in the Sydney Opera House were transported to another place.

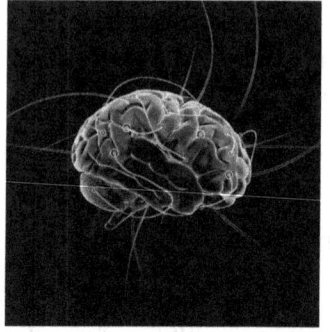 She became an invisible transmitter of sheer beauty. We were spell bound, held, till her very last note. The magical quality displayed by the great artists is indefinable. It is why we go to live concerts, to be transported. Music communicates differently, through emotion.

Below is a link to a dynamic brain scan showing the parts of the brain that are activated during the playing of a tango…..amazing. This is why classical music is taught in so many schools in Europe and throughout the world, a motto in some schools, 'Music in every class, every day'. Music has been shown to raise IQ.

Articles on music and brain activity make for interesting reading. For instance, in Alzheimer's disease the musical appreciation areas of the brain are spared.

https://www.mic.com/articles/89655
/here-s-a-surprising-look-at-what- music-does-to-your-brain

Dr. Catherine Brennan

MBBS (London), DRCOG,
Diploma of Family Planning, MRCGP,
FRACGP

General Practitioner
Trumpet, Cello, Piano

'Music is a fundamental part of who I am'

Catherine, what is your earliest musical recollection?

My earliest recollection is of my mother playing the cello. She took up playing the cello as an adult and the trigger for that was hearing Beethoven's A major cello sonata on the radio. She was so taken with it that she thought she would like to learn the cello.

How old was your mum then?

I think she must have been about 40 and I was 3.

She had some friends who used to come to our house to play string quartets. I have a memory of them playing in our lounge, but I didn't like it when she played because the cello seemed like a barrier between us. I couldn't give her a cuddle or sit on her knee because the cello got in the way. There was a lot of music in our house. My granddad was a professional oboe player and he played with the Liverpool Philharmonic Orchestra and also the Halle Orchestra in Manchester. My dad was a very keen keyboard player and the proud owner of a two manual harpsichord which he had found in a junk shop in Liverpool and then restored. Mum was also playing her cello, and my older brothers were having piano lessons, so I had a lot of exposure to music when I was little.

What age did you start learning the cello?

I started learning the cello when I was seven and the piano when I was five.

How much piano did you do before you stopped?

I had lessons up till the age of 16.

I see, so you were pretty advanced on the piano, what about the cello?

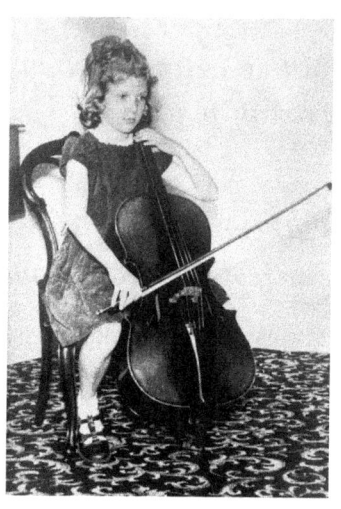

I had cello lessons until I left school.

Did you do that as a high school subject?

No, to get into medicine, you had to take all science subjects to gain entry.

When I was growing up in Liverpool the education authority awarded Music Studentships to students who were learning to play a musical instrument. You could audition for one of these and if they thought you showed promise, they would pay for you to have lessons with very good teachers, many of them players from the Liverpool Philharmonic Orchestra. I was probably about eight or nine when I first auditioned with the cello. As a condition of the studentship, you were required to attend a youth orchestra, the Liverpool Schools Symphony Orchestra, on Saturday mornings as well as re- auditioning every year. As long as they thought that you were showing progress, they would reauthorise your studentship.

That's very socialist, it's terrific.

Actually, my cello lessons were paid for by the Liverpool Educational Authority from the age of about 8 to 18. My first teacher was called Amos Moore. He had been a player in the Philharmonic Orchestra, and I really loved him. So much so that I once said to my mum 'I wish Mr. Moore was my uncle'.

When did music first speak to you?

Pretty early, I remember going to my first youth orchestra rehearsal, when I was about eight or nine, I was very nervous, and we played one of those sea shanty pieces that are always played at the Last Night of the Proms. (Fantasia on British Sea Songs - Jacks the Lad). I can remember the last page even now. I couldn't play a note of it, but when I came home, I said to my mum and dad, can I go again tomorrow?

For several years I played with the Liverpool Schools Orchestra on a Saturday morning and from the age of 11 or 12 I also played with the Merseyside Youth Orchestra on Sunday mornings. This was administered by the Liverpool Philharmonic Society, and you had to audition to get in to MYO. We had the privilege of rehearsing in the Philharmonic Hall, which is also the home of the Royal Liverpool Philharmonic Orchestra and a really beautiful concert hall. We gave 3 concerts a year there. I recently joined a Facebook group called MYO appreciation society, and somebody posted a programme from 1973. The program cost 5p which is the equivalent of about 10 cents. It was an ambitious program, which included Shostakovich 10th symphony. You can see my name right at the back of the cello section and if you look closely, you will see that the conductor was an 18 year old Simon Rattle.

Music Is Medicine

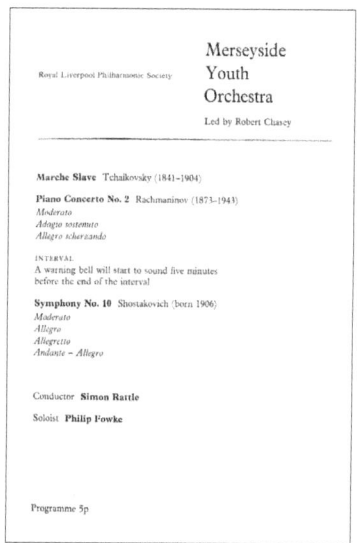

Detail from program notes above:
Simon Rattle *was born in January 1955 in Liverpool and manifested his interest in music very early. His teachers included Douglas Miller and John Ward. At the age of ten, he joined the Merseyside Youth Orchestra, of which he was a member for seven years, and later took part in many summer courses, including the National Youth Orchestra, where he received tuition in conducting from Pierre Boulez.*
Now, as a student of the Royal Academy of Music, he studied conducting under Maurice Miles and piano under Gordon Green. He has recently been appointed Chorus Master of the New Opera Company; a group affiliated to Sadler's Wells specialising in contemporary opera. In June, he will be touring Poland as pianist in a performance of Messiaen's 'Quartet for the End of Time'.

Dr. Catherine Brennan

Can you remember what would have been your most exciting musical experience as a player?

I've had several of them, but I think the most exciting was playing first trumpet in Mahler's first symphony in the Berlin Concert House with the European Doctors Orchestra. When I first listened to it with the music in front of me and looked at the last page, I laughed out loud and thought, 'I'll never be able to play that'. When it was all over, I remember leaning across to my friend Heather who was playing the second trumpet and saying, 'I don't want this night to end.' It was a very special concert.

A few years after I started playing with EDO, I was invited to play in the World Doctors Orchestra in New York. I received a rather cryptic email which said, 'Would you like to come and play the 9th symphony in Carnegie Hall?' I assumed it was referring to Beethoven's 9th. At first, I thought it might be a joke but then I contacted my friend Heather, who had received the same invitation. We agreed that we were unlikely to be invited to play in Carnegie Hall more than once and that we would both accept. So, in May 2010 we played Beethoven's 9th symphony in Carnegie Hall. A very exciting musical experience and wonderful to be able share it with such a good friend.

Now, what about as a listener?

I remember my brother Stephen taking me to a Prom concert about 10 years ago and hearing Mahler's third symphony. It was a beautiful warm and sunny early evening as we walked across Hyde Park to the Albert Hall. The symphony starts with horns and then the trombones come in early on into the piece, it was very dramatic, very special. In the third movement there is a wonderful flugelhorn solo which was played off stage from a balcony above. The beautiful, mellifluous sound seemed to float down from the heavens. That was pretty exciting.

When and why did you take up the trumpet?

I was trying to think about that earlier, I was about thirty-four when I took up the trumpet. I remember one of the first times I actually blew a note out of it and my youngest son, who was about three, clapped his hands over his ears and ran out of the room. As to the reason why, I was always a little bit fascinated by the trumpet. When I played cello in youth orchestras, I could look across to my right at the trumpet section and they usually seemed to be having a lot more fun than the cellos, and I was always curious about how you could play all the notes when you only have 3 valves. I lived in Kendal, a small market town in the north of England, and there was a little shop on the high street that sold all sorts of things, but mostly electronic gadgets.

There was a sale on, and my husband was inside spending a lot of money buying speakers and a computer chess game I seem to remember. I was standing outside waiting for him and in the window, I could see there was one flute, one trumpet and possibly a clarinet for sale. The prices were marked up on pieces of brightly coloured card cut with jagged edges and the trumpet was marked "Trumpet 99 pounds plus case". I was looking closely through the window at the trumpet and my husband was obviously feeling slightly guilty having spent so much money on things for himself when he said, 'Why don't you buy it?' I said, 'Oh, no, I'll probably never be able to play it', but he was quite insistent. So, I did, together with a Tune-a-Day book and that's how it all started.

Did you have formal trumpet lessons?

I didn't really. I worked on my Tune-a-Day book on my own at home. One of the things I did fairly early on was to take the trumpet apart, removing all the valves and slides, only to find I was completely unable to put them back in the right order. So, then I had to find somebody who could help me put it all back together again.

I had a few lessons early on with someone who was actually a trombonist. But mostly, I fumbled along on my own, and after a few years I had a few lessons with a trumpet teacher.

After playing for a year or so, I was at a school summer fete at my children's nursery school and the Burneside Brass Band came to play. I remember looking over somebody's shoulder at the second cornet part and thinking, 'I could probably play that'. I must have mentioned it to somebody who mentioned it to somebody else, and a few days later I got a call from a guy called Bill from the post office in Burneside, a small village just outside Kendal. He said, "I hear you play the trumpet", and then proceeded to tell me all about the band. By the end of the conversation, I realised that he was now expecting me to turn up on the next Tuesday night at the Burneside cricket club for rehearsal.

How big was the band?

Not very big, about 20 people.

So, the following Tuesday evening, I turned up with my trumpet, and was met by several of the players. Most of them were men from the village who worked at the local paper mill, all lovely guys and very friendly. But they took one look at my trumpet and said "Grand to see you lass, but we don't really play trumpets 'ere, we play cornets. We'll get you one." And the following week I was presented with a cornet.

What's the main difference between the Trumpet and the Cornet?

In terms of technique, it's pretty much the same, with the same fingerings and the cornet is pitched in B flat, which is the same as a B flat trumpet. However, the quality of the sound is different, the mouthpiece is smaller, but you can easily change from trumpet to cornet. I played cornet with the band for about four or five years.

Not long after I joined, preparations were being made to celebrate VJ day (Victory in Japan) 15 August. It was summertime and an announcement was made at our band practice that they needed players the following Sunday at Kirby Lonsdale, another town, not far away.

It was August and some of the regular band members from the Kirby Lonsdale band were on holiday, which meant that they would be short of cornets. I put my hand up to volunteer, not quite realising what I was letting myself in for. When I turned up on Sunday, as soon as I arrived, I was approached by one of the Kirby players who said 'Oh, we need to find you a jacket'. He rooted around in the boot of his car and produced a maroon-coloured jacket resplendent with gold braid and brass buttons, which was about four sizes too big for me, the sleeves coming down over my knuckles.

He told me that everyone was meeting in the market square, so I went to the meeting point and found lots of people in similar maroon-coloured jackets. A nice old chap said to me, "Ere luv, you go on the outside, I'm not right good at marching'.

I had never marched anywhere in my life before, and here I was on the outside of the front row of the cornets, with a jacket that was much too large for me, feeling very hot, with a small music clip-stand attached to my instrument which wobbled from side to side as I walked.

We marched from the market square, through the town and up the cobbled street to the church at the other end of the village. My music was moving from side to side due to the wobbly music stand, I was very hot in my heavy jacket, and out of breath as we made our way up hill, trying to play the music as we marched. That was one of my very few marching experiences.

Dr. Catherine Brennan

Did you go in band competitions, were you still playing the cello in an orchestra all this time?

I played cello in an orchestra, the Lakeland Sinfonia, which met three times a year and the rehearsals were tailored around those concerts, a bit like Corpus Medicorum and ADO. I also played trumpet with the Westmorland Orchestra which had weekly rehearsals in Kendal and gave three concerts a year and I was also playing in the brass band. The brass band did take part in competitions. These involved getting on a coach early on a Sunday morning and travelling to wherever the competition was being held and spending all day either listening to the other bands taking part or playing our program. And drinking quite a lot of refreshments, before setting off for home in the late afternoon. After about four years I decided I was actually doing too much, and something had to go and so I stopped playing with the brass band but I continued with the other things.

What does music mean to you?

Well, I could give you a slightly sentimental reply. I feel it is a fundamental part of who I am. Last year, when we went for so long without being able to play with friends or with an orchestra, or go to concerts and hear live music, illustrated just how much music means to me. Prior to Covid, there was always another concert on the horizon to look forward to and work towards. I found during lockdown when l listened to music, particularly to the things I had played in orchestras or chamber music, I would get very tearful.

Yes, lockdown was really miserable.

I have recently started a cello quartet. We had one rehearsal a couple of months ago, and we were meant to play again last Saturday but it had to be canceled. We rescheduled it for this Saturday, but we have had to cancel again. It is very disappointing when plans have to be called off at the last minute and very hard to arrange for four busy people to get together.

Clearly music means an awful lot to you and is a very large part of your life.

Since retiring from General Practice, music has definitely taken up a lot of my time and I find it interesting that playing two different instruments can really highlight different aspects of my personality. When I play the cello in a quartet for example, I am always playing the bass line, and the spotlight is usually shining on the upper voices.

As a cellist in an orchestra you have seven or eight other players around you to cushion and disguise any mistakes, and if you have any uncertainty you can just watch what the person next to you is doing and take the lead from them and these things appeal to my quiet and slightly introverted side. When you play the trumpet in an orchestra there is only one player to a part and you have to find the confidence to play, knowing that everyone else in the orchestra will be able to hear you. I found that very challenging when I first started playing trumpet in orchestras and often still do but I do get a tremendous adrenaline buzz, much more so when playing trumpet rather than cello.

What was going through your mind when you were playing the trumpet solo in Mahler's Blumine?

I was thinking, "If I just get this next top note then it's all plain sailing from here." I was definitely nervous when I played it.

Dr. Catherine Brennan

There's so much to that piece, firstly the quality of sound, the melody, and the phrasing. That piece is all about phrasing, the long lines, and you had it all down pat, it was a thrill to listen to.

Occasionally I hear recordings of pieces I've played with an orchestra and I am quite amazed that I was able to do it. Hearing that trumpet solo in Blumine is an example, and I find myself thinking, "Wow, did I really play that in public?"

Can you remember when things went wrong in performance?

Oh yes. When we played Mahler's first symphony, it was close, but fortunately we were able to rescue ourselves just in time. The symphony starts with four trumpets playing an off-stage fanfare. Then the players have to creep back onto the stage to join the rest of the orchestra which is already playing. After the concert I spoke to one of our friends who was in the audience. Not knowing about the off-stage fanfare, she was surprised to see the trumpets walking on stage after the symphony had started and she assumed something must have gone wrong. She thought we were late finishing our last half pint of lager in the bar and had mistimed our entrance! We crept onto the stage, being very careful not to trip over people's feet, and when I finally reached my seat, I was alarmed to find that my music wasn't on my stand.

There are about 12 bars before the 1st trumpet has an important entry. (sings trumpet tune) I turned to Heather next to me and whispered "My music is not here!" My pulse rate must have been about 120 and hers too. After some frantic rustling of pages, we found my music was on her stand and she quickly shuffled it across to me with about two beats to spare. A near disaster!

On another occasion, I was at a performance by the Liverpool Philharmonic Orchestra with a beautiful Brazilian pianist playing the Rachmaninoff's Paganini Variations. As she was getting to the end of the Cadenza, the orchestra began to pick up their instruments and get ready to come in again but somehow, she had a memory lapse and took a musical wrong turn and found herself back at the beginning of the cadenza which she proceeded to play for a second time. The players quietly put their instruments down again and waited until she had played it all through again.

Happens to the best of us, even the top professionals, that's live performance.

Oh, I can tell you a funny story about a very early performance of mine when things went wrong. When I was about six, my piano teacher entered me into a piano festival. I remember walking over to the piano which was in the middle of a very large stage in a very large hall. You could tell I was only little because when I sat down at the piano my feet didn't reach the floor and my brother Stephen was tasked with coming and putting a box under my feet. Our piano at home had a lock on the lid of the piano, and unbeknownst to anybody else this was how I identified where middle C was, because it was next to the first screw on the lock. The piano at the festival didn't have a lock. I looked at the keyboard, slightly unnerved that I could not see my usual landmark, and then started to play. The adjudicator stopped me immediately and told me that I had started on the wrong note. I had another attempt at finding the right place to start, but it took three goes and eventually he had to come up on stage, pointed to the correct note and said, "Start there."

Needless to say, I didn't win a prize. (Both of us have a really good laugh.)

Dr. Catherine Brennan

What would be your desert island discs?

I'd have to have the complete Bach Solo Cello Suites and Mahler's first symphony, including the Blumine movement. Beethoven string quartet opus 132 and the Mozart C major quintet, as well as Richard Strauss's Alpine Symphony. I might also need a Shostakovich symphony. I just have to choose between 5, 10, 15 and 7, the Leningrad Symphony and the Rite of Spring.

How much do you practise?

That varies. At the beginning of the first lockdown, when it was only meant to last for six weeks, I told myself that if I practised the cello and the trumpet for 20 minutes each day then at the end of six weeks, I would be a much better player. 20 minutes isn't very much, and normally I would do more than that, but in actual fact, after only a few days, I ended up doing nothing at all.I, like you, find it hard to practice without a target. At the moment I am doing a bit of cello, a bit of trumpet and a bit of piano pretty much most days.

Well, that explains a lot of things because I've heard you play those three instruments beautifully. Is there anything you'd like to say about the doctors' orchestras.

The first time I played with the doctor's orchestra was in 2011 and I've played in most concerts since then. Taking up the trumpet was one of the best things I've ever done because, in Kendal, there weren't really any other trumpeters, so I had many opportunities to play in a symphony orchestra. When EDO (European Doctors Orchestra) gave their first concert, I remember ringing Stephen my brother one Sunday evening. Sam, his son picked up the phone and told me that Stephen was out somewhere playing his violin. I found this quite surprising because

I knew he hadn't played for years. That was the first EDO concert, November 2004. When I spoke to Stephen about it, he suggested that I should apply for the next concert and I played in all the concerts after that, both in London and overseas until I moved to Australia. Through EDO, I have been able to travel throughout Europe and I have met some lovely people who have become good friends and it's just been a hugely enriching thing to have done.

The same can be said about ADO. I have visited all the state capital cities in Australia with the exception of Darwin, having only moved here in 2013. I have made some very good friends and have had the chance to be a part of some incredible performances in some famous concert halls and it has provided many opportunities and memorable experiences for me. I think that after Covid, when we are able to come together again to play music it will seem all the more special.

Dr Peter Purches

MB,BS Hons. Dip. obs.RCOG FRACGP, Grad. Dip. HSM

General Practitioner
Violin, Trombonee, Arranger

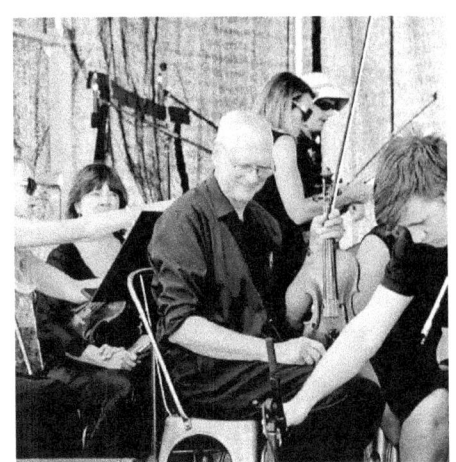

'Music means more to me now than it ever did'

What are your earliest musical recollections?

When I was eight, I started playing the violin at Linden Park School in Adelaide. I was taught by Mr. Bill Haydock who was a fiddle player with the Adelaide symphony for years and we then went to Sydney when I was 10.

In Sydney I continued to have lessons until I graduated from high school with Miss Nancye McGilchrist. The trombone came about because I was at Balgowlah Boys High, and we had a visiting bandmaster called Reg Bishop. I expressed interest in joining the band and he chose a trombone for me because I had the longest arms of all the boys on the day. I was 12.

I continued with my violin lessons and did the AMEB exams reaching seventh grade. The good thing about that was that I could do music as an extra subject in the HSC, so I did 7th. grade violin and sixth grade theory, that along with a thesis on British 20th century choral music got me a level one music pass which in turn helped get me into medicine.

I had a 10 year hiatus not playing much between starting uni and starting my first country general practice in West Wyalong in 1978. I played casually in West Wyalong, in little cameos like Fiddler on the

Roof, and playing in the West Wyalong Town Band. When I started in Wagga, it was on for young and old, there was a lot of music there.

Music in Wagga was terrific, there was a Conservatorium and a concert band, so I played in both. We also had a little quartet for hire, and we played at weddings every weekend. Then later in Wagga, I met John Ansell, a famous jazz musician who had a band called the Riverina Jazz Band and they were short of a trombone player and got me in.

I was a beginner at that, but they persevered with me till I learnt to play from the chords. That was a great part of my life, playing jazz every weekend, doing balls and things like that. It was a time when trad jazz was at its peak but then fell away. Our band used to go all over New South Wales and Victoria participating in jazz festivals. It was a great time. The people who were fans of that sort of music simply thinned out, the music was a relic of the sixties.

Can you remember when music first spoke to you?

I find it hard to answer that because I've never had a time in my life when music wasn't a part of my life, it was always there. Music making in the country was convivial and people helped and supported each other, and the same in Sydney playing with Mosman Orchestra, Manly Brass Band and a bush- rock band, 'The Ducks'.

Whose idea was it for you to play the violin?

It was my idea. My father was a person who just reacted instantly to anything like that. He wasn't a musician nor was mum, but I said, 'I want to learn the violin', and the next day there was a violin for me.

Dr Peter Purches

What was your most exciting musical experience as a player and as a listener?

As a player, it was playing jazz because it took me everywhere. I had a great time, a mixture of social interaction and great playing. I did that for eight years.

I reached a standard that I could play trad jazz, reading the chords and supplying a solo when required.

When I turned 60, I decided to have trombone lessons for the first time. I never really studied the trombone, I just played it. I took lessons with Jeff Power, a famous jazz man around Sydney, he is a Conservatorium graduate and a very well-rounded musician. I did seventh and the eighth grade AMEB trombone exams. I was starting to do A.Mus.A because that was always a goal of mine, but I faltered, and it fell by the wayside.

As a listener there's been so many things that reached me that way. The most spectacular thing that I've heard was when we went to Europe in 1997 and we went to the Concertgebouw in

Peter on trombone enjoying playing with his trad jazz band

Amsterdam. We were hoping to get a ticket, and we got the last two. They asked us with two other couples to go onto the stage. We sat right behind the Borodin string quartet. I can never forget that, but the hardest part was sitting still and not giving any indication that you were a part of the show. I was looking straight over the second violinist's shoulder, and I could read the music. Apparently, they did this when the hall was full.

What does music mean to you?

Well, I think it means more to me now than it ever did. I'm spending a lot of time recording and arranging things for piano which I never used to do much, as work and family consumed any time I had left. This is my biggest interest now, especially during lockdown, you can't go out and play music so you might as well do it at home.

I like doing it, we have done some interesting things over the internet, I've arranged some pieces and then others have contributed from their different homes via the net. For example, I play fiddle with bush band, and we've put tunes together where a few of us play together and then someone contributes from Dubbo, others join in from the central coast then we put it all together. It's very creative and fun.

The last thing I arranged was a song called 'Too Late Now'. It's a 1930s tune and I did it with myself on vocals, which is my weak link, because I couldn't get anyone else to do it, and put a violin and viola obligato behind it. Then I sent it to my mate in Wingham, and he added a wonderful guitar part. Music technology is excellent these days, and I use a home recording studio to assemble these pieces.

Can you remember when things went wrong in the performance?

Something always goes wrong in a performance, but the whole always seems better than the sum of the parts.

I play second violin in the orchestra now because there are more trombonists. Over time, there are more brass and wind players than in the early days of ADO, and everyone needs to have a chance.

Tell us about the conducting part of your music making.

I conducted the junior concert band in Wagga for a year or so. One of the early band members in Wagga was Peter Mews, who now works as a neurosurgeon in Canberra and plays trombone in ADO when he can. I have never forgotten Peter nailing the trombone solo in Ravel's Bolero in an ADO concert on the Sunshine Coast, and since then have maintained that I taught him well when he was a youngster.

What are your desert island choices?

Fauré's Piano Quartet, number one.

I always play chamber music at home, so I guess any of the chamber works. In jazz, I love Benny Goodman, especially his small groups.

How did you discover ADO?

Elizabeth Millard put me on to it when I was in Wagga. I think that it's been the prime musical experience playing wise in my life, I've loved it. The ADO is special, what else can you say about it? It's an opportunity to hear and play with some good musicians and there are so many of those in the orchestra. The best thing about ADO is that you can be busy at work and get a big dose of music in one or two weekends a year. Thank you, Miki, for starting the whole show.

Bronwyn Francis

MBBS (Hons) FRACP

Paediatrician, Violin, Viola

'Music is sentimental, powerful, humorous, inspirational and everything in-between'

What was your earliest musical recollection?

My Mother, Nan Francis was a professional violinist, my father loved music. I was exposed to music from a very early age. I remember wanting to play the violin when I was two. My mother used to allow me to play her violin, I badgered her till I was six and then I was allowed to have my own violin, that was my start.

Mother was always giving recitals, conducting orchestras and teaching the violin. She had been a member of the MSO, and when I was young, we watched her playing in the "Music for the People" symphony concerts at the Myer Music Bowl. Mum taught me till I was a teenager but then we had too many fights during the lessons. She bailed and then I went to study with Jean Lehmann and later with Nathan Gutmann.

My father was an engineer at the Australian Paper Mills, initially in Gippsland and later Mt Gambier. Every fortnight I would fly from Mount Gambier to Melbourne to have violin lessons.

Can you remember when music first spoke to you?

I can't because it was there from the beginning. I remember really enjoying the times with the National and State Music Camps, loving the social side as well as the music.

It was quite a big thing for a country girl to attend the National Music Camp because virtually no one else from my high school played the violin. I certainly couldn't share my secret passion with anyone else.

When I was born my mother had to leave the MSO, actually, in those in those days women who got married were made casual. You lost your permanent position because women weren't given the same opportunities as men. She was always being called in when people were sick.

Opportunities for women were wiped out the minute they got engaged. When she got engaged, she couldn't wear her ring because she didn't want anyone to know and risk losing her position, she was engaged for six years. Then they got married and I took six years to come along. We moved to the country when I was two and she literally lost her professional career then and became a mother and an educator, she was trained as a teacher.

What was your most exciting musical experience first as a player and then as a listener?

I have vivid memories of playing Shostakovich's Fifth Symphony with the Australian Youth Orchestra. I was overwhelmed by the power of the music and the fact that I was right in the midst of it. It was emotionally exhilarating. Later that year we played Tchaikovsky's Fourth Symphony, and I was caught, hook, line, and sinker.

We had great conductors, John Hopkins, Robert Pickler and John Curro, they were brilliant and inspiring musicians.

I considered a career in music and given another chance I would pursue the combined 'Music- Medicine' degrees now offered. My mother was the one who influenced me in choosing Medicine. 'You can always play the violin as a doctor, but you can't easily be a doctor when you're a musician.' I am fortunate and grateful that I can pursue both my passions, Music, and Medicine.

Music Is Medicine

As a listener I can remember hearing Jessye Norman singing in the Melbourne Town Hall. My parents had been to the concert the night before and they were so moved that they paid for the whole family to see it again.

The other occasion, when I was five, we saw 'The Barber of Seville'. Apparently, I was completely entranced, singing along with the performers.

I was in orchestras from the age of eight and this cutting is from the Traralgon Journal.

What does music mean to you?

Music is about expression. It is communication from within myself. It's the way I feel things, it's more powerful than words. Music can make me cry, more often than anything else. I find tears running down my face when I am playing or listening to music.

We've had some beautiful moments over the years, the tap is right there, reaching our deepest emotions. Music is sentimental, powerful, humorous and inspirational and everything in between.

Can you remember when things went wrong in a performance?

We were playing a Brahms Piano Concerto and our soloist was playing from memory and got lost. Our conductor, Keith Crellin, kept conducting, with confidence, all the same it was a scary moment because then we were all completely lost.

What are your Desert Island choices?

Jessye Norman singing Richard Strauss' 'Last Four Songs', and the second movement of Beethoven's Seventh Symphony. the Beethoven String Quartets as well as symphonies by Shostakovich, Schubert, Mendelssohn and Mahler.

Do you like orchestral or chamber music or both?

I like it all, however playing music and experiencing it from within really makes me love it even more. Orchestral music is wonderful because of the numerous colours of all the instruments. I love hearing the French horns, and trumpets, the haunting melodies from the oboes and the bassoons. One of the more difficult experiences I've had was being too close to the shrill sounds of the piccolo, giving me tinnitus!

I remember talking to Chris Martin who was going quite deaf in his last few years, saying that a lot of musicians go deaf because of the constant noise surrounding them.

'Yes, but what a nice way to go deaf' was his reply.

How much do you practise?

At times I am addicted to practising for many hours every day. In recent years I have been having lessons with Paul Wright who is an amazing teacher. He inspired me to play a repertoire that I had previously considered too difficult and to produce the best sound from my violin which was made by the famous A.E. Smith.

Which were your most memorable musical moments?

I've been fortunate to be able to participate in the Mt Buller Summer School, some years have been very special. The most memorable was when our quartet achieved a balanced and blended sound, playing with friends, communicating with music is a sublime experience.

I've had fabulous, musically fulfilling times playing with ADO, and I've been so incredibly fortunate to have made musical friendships with like-minded colleagues. We've managed to play a huge repertoire of orchestral music, and I am especially pleased to have participated in the violin and viola sections of the orchestra.

It has given so much enjoyment by making music in a big setting of the orchestra. How many other people get that in their professional life? We are just so lucky. The standard has mostly been excellent. Not every time, but you know what I mean? So, as you look back there's always been some waxing and waning in the standard, but essentially the experience has always been wonderful.

When I reflect on my career choice to become a doctor, rather than a musician, I feel extremely fortunate to have still had incredible musical opportunities throughout my life.

How lucky is that?

Phillip Antippa OAM
MBBS, FRACS

Cardio Thoracic Surgeon, Melbourne
Principal Founding Viola, ADO Founder of Corpus Medicorum

'Music is an incredible addiction that's almost impossible to feed, so you look for those incredible moments every time you play to feed the addiction.'

I first met Phillip while he was training as a young surgeon almost 30 years ago. Phillip was involved right at the start of ADO in 1993. With his enormous organisational skills and energy, together with Anaesthetist Rowan Thomas, founding concertmaster, we forged ADO.

At one of our very first meetings, I couldn't help noticing a little metal ingot that was attached to Phillip's key ring, it read "Damn I'm Good". Such subjective insights are rarely true, but in Phillips's case they proved to be correct. He is an excellent surgeon as well as an excellent violist and section leader.

Phillip led ADO's viola section for 16 years. Not only that, he took on many other organisational tasks, not least of which was that of ADO librarian. In the era before emails, that meant copying reams of parts for a 100-piece orchestra. No small feat, it also entailed buying or hiring original parts. Original parts have to be used in public performances, to comply with the law and to ensure royalties go to the composers and publishers.

As in all good ethnic (Greek) families he was encouraged (made) to play the piano from the age of 5.

"Can you remember the first-time music spoke to you?'

My mother took me down to Mrs. Harris for lessons, she was very old and grumpy. The lessons were always on a Friday afternoon. I distinctly remember sitting in her 'smelly' front room. She had a ruler and if you made a mistake, she'd whack you over the knuckles with it. So, my first musical memories were not particularly happy. I wasn't a particularly talented piano player, but I stuck with it and completed all my AMEB grades.

When I was seven or eight, my parents sent me to an expensive school where I was put in the orchestra and a violin shoved in my hands. I enjoyed that and found it fun. Then after a few years they needed a viola player for the senior orchestra, and I was asked to join that. I had just played a Bach piece in my piano exam and when I got home my old man had just bought me a synthesiser. I played the Bach on it, and I just thought, that's incredible. This piece which was torture on the piano had another voice and it just meant something entirely different.'

A great early musical moment was playing in the orchestra. I had only been playing the viola for five or six months and we played Schostakovich's fifth Symphony. It was the scariest and most amazing thing I'd ever struck. All of a sudden it was a lightbulb moment realising what that music was.

Music is an incredible addiction that's almost impossible to feed, so you look for those incredible moments every time you play to feed the addiction.

I remember playing Sibelius' 2nd Symphony with Keith Crellin conducting. We were all playing at our limit, there were wrong notes for sure, but the music was so great it didn't matter. You could feel that everyone was there and fully committed, going for it. There is nothing like that feeling in earth or in heaven.

Phillip Antippa OAM

Tell me about the founding Corpus Medicorum.

Basically, even though I enjoyed ADO very much it was only one concert a year. I knew Chris Martin very well as I had a bursary with him studying the viola at the Conservatorium. I also wanted to expand the repertoire and play more challenging pieces.

We started with a string orchestra and built on that. With Keith (Crellin) we could be adventurous and play Shostakovich, Vaughan Williams, Mahler and Rachmaninoff.

Do you share your musical passion with your patients?'

'When a patient asks me 'How can we ever thank you doctor?'

'I'll say, well, come to our concerts. I'll put you on our email list. And you know there are 50-60 patients who regularly come to our concerts.'

What does music mean to you in your life?'

As you know, to be a surgeon you need to give an extraordinary piece of your life to it. But you have to be careful not to let it be all consuming.

We've all colleagues who have work as the only thing in their life, and when they stop working there is nothing.

Music juxtaposes the level of commitment you have for your work. So, it's a perfect balance. Whenever I experience problems in my life, be that work or family, music is what releases me from that.

There is no time to think of anything else when you are playing music. Music has the ability to capture my entire being. That's just how it is.'

Dr. Cathy Fraser

MB,ChB (University of Cape Town)
Masters in general Practice Psychiatry (Monash),
FACPM (Fellow of the Australian College of Psychological Medicine)

General Practitioner, Flute, Piccolo

'Music sings to me, the flute is my voice. It's part of life, I cannot imagine life without it, it's part of being human. It is a language of emotion and expression, it's in me all the time.'

What is your earliest musical recollection?

Practising the piano. My mother was a piano teacher, and I grew up with the discipline of being woken at six thirty every morning, going straight to the piano before I did anything else. I was about 6 years old then. When we got back from school, the piano was not available because she was giving lessons on it.

Did you have siblings who were also learning an instrument?

Yes, my sister had the 7:00 AM slot, so I grew up with the discipline of half an hour piano practice every morning. Later I wanted to play a second instrument other than the recorder which I'd played for years. I just loved the sound of the flute. For my 14th birthday, I can still remember unwrapping my first flute. I donated it to the Australian Children's Music Foundation yesterday and finally parted with it.

Can you remember when music spoke to you?

Emotional memories, where you are moved and can even become tearful, stand out. I recall Samuel Barber's Adagio for Strings bringing me to tears at a chamber music camp. It wasn't the best performance, but the music really spoke to me. I was sitting directly behind the conductor right in front of the first violins. I felt I was actually in the music.

What made you take up the flute?

I love the sound of the flute. Something about it, it has a singing quality. I am also learning the cello which I took up three years ago. Interestingly there are lots of flautists who also play the cello. There's something about the cello and the flute that is in common, whether it's romantic or emotional or moving, but to me they both sing. Whenever I listen to orchestral music it's always the flute that I notice. I feel that's my voice.

Did you finish all your grades on the piano?

Yes, but after I left home aged 17, I didn't play the piano regularly as the flute was more portable. I finished my grades on the flute while I was a medical student.

What was your most exciting musical experience as a player?

That would be playing in the Australian Doctors Orchestra for the first time (much laughter). Having had a break from playing with other musicians, after going through studying and working, to actually be able to get together with colleagues and mix it with music was precious and life changing.

What about as a listener?

As a listener, it was the first performance of the Australian World Orchestra held in Sydney Opera House with Simone Young conducting. My flute teacher Emma Sholl was playing in the flute section. I was sitting at the side of the stage, watching like an excited little kid.

What does music mean to you?

It's part of life, I cannot imagine life without music, it's part of being human. It is a language of emotion and expression, it's in me all the time.

In what ways has it helped you in your medical life?

Music has helped in terms of general traits, such as discipline, conscientiousness, memory, focus, and working towards goals. Traits that help both in working in music and enjoying it and working in medicine and enjoying it.

How and why did you start Musicus Medicus in Sydney?

I started it in 2004 just one year after Phillip Antippa started Melbourne's Corpus Medicorum. If Melbourne is doing it, Sydney has to follow.

Further expanding her Musicus Medicus orchestral and other activities.

Like ADO, in addition to fund raising for a different medical charity annually, Musicus Medicus has collaborated with Sydney Eisteddfod since 2009 to fund a "Sydney Eisteddfod NSW Doctors Orchestra Instrumental Scholarship" (16-25 years) for $15000 a year.

Cathy personally sponsors the annual prize for the Premium Youth Orchestra (19 and under). She has become an advocate for young people, promoting their engagement in music as a lifelong aspiration, encouraging them to keep playing, even if they don't choose music as a profession. A lot of her time in general practice was spent with young children and families, and then in her psychotherapy practice, she helped adolescents in turmoil. It was a natural progression to share her message to young people on a speech circuit, including AMEB, schools and music clubs. She promotes 'creative health' as an essential part of a good work life balance and stresses the importance of keeping up creative interests in combination with study and work. She stated, "there are times when we need to put our instruments down but having something specific to work towards, as we do in our Doctors Orchestras, can be motivating, it gives us opportunities for memorable and meaningful experiences.

The NSW Doctors Orchestra (Musicus Medicus) had to cancel planned concerts three times due to Covid-related restrictions. Because of the prolonged time between concerts, Cathy has arranged chamber music soirees at her home, as well as online interactive workshops helping players keep in touch with their musical side.

How many ADO concerts have you played in?

Most of them so it's easier for me to say which ones I've missed.

How long were you ADO president?

Four years and then Mike Eaton from Perth took over. When invited to be president and take over because the current president was going to London (you were going to London), I said, 'what?' I was shocked, and initially said, 'I couldn't do that!' But it was life transforming, it built my confidence, and made me realise I had strengths that other people could see that I wasn't acknowledging. I can't imagine life without ADO which has shaped my life. As an immigrant to this country, it's been a great way to meet like-minded people from all over Australia.

We started in ADO in '93. So, it was seven, eight years after I had arrived in 1985.

How many ADO concerts did you organise?

I've lost count, probably five.

How often does Musicus Medicus perform?

Usually once, sometimes twice, a year. Next year we'll organise two concerts to make up for this Covid year.

What would be your desert island discs choices?

It would have to be to be Mozart. He was so prolific, I would have to include his flute and harp concerto, but it's so hard to choose. I would also go for variety, so I would include an Australian composer such as Peter Sculthorpe with a bit of jazz thrown in. Something with Don Burrows to bring back happy memories and I would want a mixture of orchestral and solo work as well. I adore Miriam Hyde's compositions, I play all her flute sonatas, there are five of them.

Do you play any chamber music?

I do, I play more chamber music than orchestral.

Who do you play with and with what other instruments?

We have an incredibly active chamber music society here in Sydney and I've played with them for 30 years, that's how I first heard about ADO. Other than that, I've played regularly in a wind quintet and in a wind trio with a bassoon and a cello. A local composer composes for us. I also often play flute duets with a fellow flautist.

In what way has ADO been life-changing for you?

ADO has shaped my life, it's been such a vital part, not just as a source of music, but also for building character and drawing on strengths and growing self-confidence. Then there is the social side, meeting a variety of people of different ages and from different places, as well as different disciplines of medicine. It's been fantastic, I am very grateful.

Andrew Kennedy (ADO Clarinettist) and I played duets at a harpist's 60th birthday recently and standing right in front of me was Jane Rutter, world famous concert flautist. Talk about coping with daunting experiences! Afterwards she said, 'Well done'.

You organised the 25th ADO concert in Sydney, it was an overwhelming success.

It was loads of fun with Nicholas Milton conducting Shostakovich's 10th Symphony. He's keen to conduct us again too. The other wonderful thing about ADO is that it introduces us to professionals who have enjoyed collaborating with us. It breaks down the barriers between amateurs and professionals. It's added spice to our lives.

The Violin As a Passport

MJP

Playing the violin is a marvelous hobby has allowed me to visit 3 continents as well as many cities and towns throughout Australia. It has been my passport, allowing me to enter people's lives, make lifelong friends and share the love of music with like-minded people.

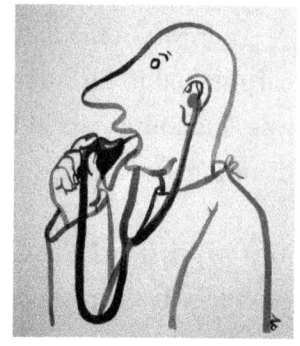

The violin has transported me, both physically and emotionally on many occasions with European Doctors Orchestra (EDO), Corpus Medicorum, Associated Chamber Music Players (ACMP), World Doctor's Orchestra (WDO). I have been lucky to play and tour Taiwan, China, France, Poland, Italy, Germany, Norway, Russia, Romania, Hungary, Slovenia, Ireland, UK, USA and Canada.

The European Doctors Orchestra (EDO)

We were rehearsing Mahler's Second Symphony in Belfast with EDO for a Sunday evening concert in the City Hall. We start rehearsals on Thursday night and work all through Friday and then Saturday morning.

We finally arrived at Saturday afternoon's rehearsal when the soloists make their first appearance with us. Everyone is always excited and there is a buzz in the air. The fourth movement of Mahler 2 requires a Mezzo-Soprano and a Soprano. The two soloists were both from Derry, unknown to us. I had listened to just about every recording of this symphony as I am sure had most of the rest of the orchestra. Expectations were high.

You must understand that by Saturday afternoon we had been rehearsing for 2 days, not to mention the obligatory partying at night. We were exhausted, emotions were tenderised as with a meat tenderising hammer.

The Mezzo-soprano was of generous proportions, (singers often seem to be that shape), the Soprano, however, was of a delicate slender build. 'A wee slip of a girl' as the Irish would have it. The tune for the fourth movement is taken from Mahler's 'Das Knaben Wunderhorn' (Youth's Magic Horn). It's about man dying and entering God's arms in heaven, hence the symphony's nickname, 'Resurrection Symphony'.

The Mezzo begins first, she had a beautiful robust voice, but then ……….. the Soprano began the main theme……….WOW!

We were all thunderstruck. How could such a delicately proportioned body produce THAT volume a n d quality of sound. Her singing was sublime, better than anything I had heard on any recording.

Some wept so hard that they couldn't continue to play. Others just cried and kept playing. Others just teared up. As a surgeon I am a fairly hard-nosed bastard, but I must confess, I fell into this last category and teared up. The secret to avoid detection is not to wipe your eyes, just let the tears flow down your cheeks uninterrupted. Wiping them away is a dead giveaway.

China with Jan Sedivka, 1988

In 1988 I went with Jan Sedivka to China. He had been invited as Professor of Violin to the prestigious Shanghai Conservatorium. My role could be best described as his 'Boy Friday'. I considered this a pleasure and a great honour. We were invited to hear Qin Li Wei, a 10-year-old cellist, now internationally famous and known as just 'LIWEI'. His father was a cellist in the Shanghai Symphony Orchestra and En Pei, his mother was rumored to be the finest pianist in China. She was on a scholarship in Hobart.

We were ushered into a small bedroom with two single beds facing each other, the room was lit with one neon tube. Li Wei entered carrying a half-sized cello, bowed in a very dignified way for a ten- year-old and sat down, then, with no fuss at all, began to play one of J. S. Bach's solo cello suites. The music and artistry emanating from this child were unbelievable. We all knew we were in the presence of greatness; this boy was a 'transmitter' directly from JS 300 years ago to us. When he finished no one stirred. We were all so moved that there was total silence for a whole minute, and everyone had a tear in their eyes, even Jan who was known not to be easily moved!

Charles Sturt University Summer String School, Wagga Wagga

Our four boys were all learning stringed instruments. Nick cello, Will violin, Charlie viola and Erik the Double Bass. Chris Martin had invited us to the Summer String School that he conducted annually at the Charles Sturt University in Wagga Wagga. Over the years we became enthusiastic participants. Chris would often ask me to lead the orchestra which comprised children, adolescents and parents who also wanted to play. It was always nerve-racking to lead because if I jumped over a cliff they would follow without any hesitation.

My reward finally came. The string tutors were all Chris's old mates who had had illustrious careers. They included the great Carl Pini who was concertmaster of the Philharmonia Orchestra in London at the age of 21. He had actually worked with Sir Thomas Beecham who helped him buy his first really good violin. The other was Don Hazelwood, who had been the revered Concertmaster of the Sydney Symphony for many years. As an aside, during a rehearsal Don would sit in with the children at the back of the second violin section helping out. A little girl aged 9 sitting in front of him heard him play, she turned around and said: 'Jeeez you're good' Don's reply was the greatest demonstration of graciousness I have ever heard. 'Thank you, Dear'.

Now back to the thrust of my story. Chris decided that we could utilise two great talents and we would play Vivaldi's 'Concerto for Two Violins' with Don and Carl as soloists. The usual arrangement for that piece is to have the two soloists in front of stage, next to the conductor's podium, but to my absolute delight, they sat in the front desks. As I was leading, all I had to do was move one seat left, placing me next to the now leader Carl Pini on my right and immediately on my left was the now leader of the seconds, Don Hazelwood. I was sandwiched between two of my heroes, giants in music. Nick, Will and Charlie said I had a fixed grin on my face the whole time we were playing the Vivaldi.

Carl Pini, MJP, Donald Hazelwood (L to R) Wagga Wagga, 1999 Music Camp

Associate Chamber Music Players (ACMP), New York

Associate Chamber Music Players was founded in New York. It's an organisation allowing fellow amateur musicians to arrange chamber music sessions when away from home. Arranging a session is quite straight forward. Mary and I went to New York to see our oldest son who was on a high school exchange. Before leaving Australia, I looked up the ACMP International Register and found Margaret Saltonstall, ACMP's founder. Her own ensemble String Quartet played for their own enjoyment in a famous music venue 'The Barge' which was situated at the foot of Brooklyn Bridge. On Monday nights The Barge was closed to the public but Olga and Margaret with two others played string quartets. I had emailed ahead, it was set, I was to sit in as their second violin for the night.

Olga Bloom who owned and managed 'The Barge'. She was a retired member of the New York Philharmonic and the quartet's leader. Before bow is put to string, the atmosphere is quite tense. All sorts of panicky ideas raced through my mind, I've never played with these people before, what is the standard, can I cut it with the New Yorkers? As soon as the music starts, all is well, and we can begin to enjoy ourselves.

After the obligatory stiff introductions, and even before we were seated, I heard the pop of a cork and wine being poured.

'Oh, you have wine at the *start* of your rehearsals?'

'Oh yes, we find it the best part, don't you' replied Olga. I knew I was in for a good night and relaxed.

Olga made the most beautiful silky, full-bodied, luscious sound.

In the break between movements, I couldn't contain myself any longer.

'Olga, that is the most wonderful-sounding violin. It must be Italian. What is it?' 'Oh, it's a Guarneri, would you like to play it?'

I had the best time playing that marvelous instrument but as soon as we finished the slow movement, I carefully handed it back to her. I was very conscious of how valuable it must have been, in the millions. It was particularly generous of Olga to let me play it, the finest instrument I have ever played.

I have had similar experiences with ACMP members in Canada, Hungary, Ireland, and the UK. They are always a bit scary at first but end up being rewarding, notably my Hungarian ACMP encounter.

ACMP, Budapest

Two days before leaving for Budapest, I emailed Tamás Geszti, a violinist/violist who also happened to be a professor of physics at the Eötvös University. He replied immediately. He phoned my hotel the day after we arrived at 7 am the morning. There was a knock at the door. The man standing in front of me was holding a violin and some sheet music tucked under his arm.

'Hello, Miklós.'

'Tamás, is this your violin?' 'Yes, of course, why?'

'Well, we've never met, and you are lending me your violin."

'Ah well, I did look you up on the net after you rang. I'll pick you up at 7 tonight. Is that OK?' 'Great, see you then.'

We had a wonderful night playing through quartets with two professionals. When they left at about 10.30

Tamás turned to me and said… 'Do you want to play some duets?' 'Sure.'

We played till 2 am.

He invited me to join his orchestra the following evening for a rehearsal. He played viola, allowing me to play his violin. When I arrived, his violin was waiting for me on a seat in the first violin section. We played Mozart, a Haydn Symphony and Leo Weiner's Divertimento, a charming piece which I had not played before. Luckily, I was familiar with the other pieces. The orchestra was of a high standard, and I really enjoyed myself. My deskie was a young mathematics student.

At the end of that rehearsal Tamás suggested I come to rehearse with another orchestra at Mátyás Templom (St Matthew's Cathedral) the following night. The Cathedral is in the Buda Hills, with very beautiful views of the Danube, next to the Castle and Fisherman's Bastion. All the Kings and Queens of Hungary had been crowned there for the past 600 years. I arrived at the Cathedral and began to look for the artists' galley entrance. I finally found a tiny spiral staircase at the back of the church that led straight into the musicians' loft, four flights up. I was made to feel welcome straight away. Their conductor was also the conductor of the Budapest Doctors' Orchestra. It was a joy making music with my countrymen in such a historic setting. We rehearsed Mozart's Krönungsmesse (Coronation Mass).

Music is 'The' international language, no barriers.

In Budapest, more than anywhere else, I felt privileged to be able to step into the inner circle of music- making at such short notice. Having been born there, and still having the language, certainly helped.

Blind Cow Pottery, Marong, Victoria

Off the grid, Blind Cow Pottery was built of mud brick by Deidre Outhred and Ray Pearce. Deidre is a painter and Ray a famous potter. The house is huge, comprising a performance space, bedrooms, kitchen, living space and an amazing turret.  We set up on an open verandah at the side of the house. On the day of the concert there were large fire pits that had been lit in the garden, nestled amongst the gum trees where the audience were seated under the stars, on chairs and sofas, all from the local tip shop.

Audience and performers nestled in the magnificent Australian Bush.

The Violin As a Passport

We were billed with a tap dancer, a jazz-blues singer and a piece of electronic music played by the composer on his computer. We took up the whole second half of the programme performing Mozart's massive 45 minute long G. Minor Viola Quintet.

Old carpet runners were laid on the dirt in the aisles between the chairs and as it was the Anzac Day weekend, old posters of WWI scenes were projected onto the turret walls above us, creating an absolutely magical atmosphere.

Our music stands were lit by battery-driven sconce lights. Our audience's taste was diverse, and this type of classical music was new to them. During the second movement the generators failed and there was an audible stir. With our fully acoustic (nonelectric) instruments and our battery driven lights, we didn't skip a beat, everyone thought we would have to stop, but we didn't of course. The audience was exceptionally quiet throughout the 45 minutes as they were drawn into the music.

Comments like, 'None of you stopped during the blackout' and 'You were all moving your bows in the same direction at one point', followed.

It's a pleasure for us to be able to introduce great music to an audience that hasn't been exposed to it before. We can hardly wait for Covid restrictions to lift as Deidre and Ray have installed an old Melbourne tram on their property which will be the backdrop to our new stage, the audience will still be seated in the bush in front of us.

Deidre and Ray enjoying their latest acquisition, a vintage Melbourne tram.

Benjamin Martin

Concert Pianist, ADO Soloist

'Piano is my sanity, it's the tactile relationship with Airwaves and Sound'

A conversation with Benjamin Martin (Pianist) about music and his father Christopher Martin (ADO's, musical director and inaugural Conductor)

Benjamin Martin

M: You've been our ADO soloist on three occasions and of course your father Chris was our founding conductor. Chris and I met at the 1993 Mt Buller Summer Camp for Strings, and we struck up an immediate friendship. Also at that camp was Rowan Thomas who became our first Concert Master, a position that he held for 12 years. You have also been the soloist with Phillip Antippa's Corpus Medicorum, but could

we focus on ADO? They were in 2011, 2002 and 1997, all in Sydney. The two memorable ones were the 2002 concert when we played Beethoven's Triple concerto with Libby Wallfisch, violin and Niall Brown as our cello. The other one that looms large in my mind was the Grieg Piano Concerto in 1997. After the Grieg, the great Carl Pini[3] said to your father:

'I don't think I'll ever hear that more beautifully played.'

---

3   Carl Pini: Past concertmaster of Royal Philharmonic Orchestra and Melbourne Symphony Orchestra

B: 'I didn't know that. That means a great deal to me.'

I haven't seen Carl for a long time, it's so hard to get to see anybody at home these days.

M: Beethoven's Triple Concerto was with a very big orchestra. There was an extra dimension to Chris that wasn't appreciated in his lifetime because he was very humble and self-effacing. A few who knew the gift he had, when he asked Niall Brown to be the Cellist. 'I chose Niall because he has a wonderful upper register on the instrument and that's what's needed for the triple.'

B: Dad was primarily an aesthete, everything had to be of the highest order of taste. Or for him it was vulgar. He had an extremely developed aesthetic sense.

He had incredibly fine sensibilities that actually tyrannised him.

When he went to play golf with Simon (Ben's brother), and Simon was about to hit off he said: 'Greg Norman, he'd get it on the green in one.'

A part of his perfectionism which interfered a lot with his life. His perfectionist attitude occasionally took the fun out of life.

M: His sense of humour gave a joyous feeling to the orchestra; he really knew how to get the best out of us.

B: You knew Dad so well. It was that sense of love in the true meaning of amateur, right? The sense of something for the sake of it. There was a conflict in him because he had such high standards, which were professional rather than amateur. At the same time, he gravitated towards the love of the amateur and made sure not to try to professionalize the orchestra. He vacillated between the two.

M: Essentially, he was a self-trained conductor, wasn't he?

B: To the best of my knowledge, he never had any formal training as a conductor. That's not to say that he didn't take it incredibly seriously.

M: He told me that when he was working with the New Edinburgh Quartet and with Simon Goldberg in Holland, he formed the Christopher Martin Chamber Orchestra which continued long after he left.

He was annoyed that he was never awarded an Order of Australia, but then you have to be an Australian citizen to be eligible. He never took out Australian citizenship, and used to say repeatedly, 'British is best'.

B: The question of feeling appreciated bridged a number of areas in his life. At the same time a part of him had no time for those kinds of awards and ceremonies.

There was a paradox in him that both wanted to be acknowledged for his artistic contribution, which after all is perfectly human, and yet having a real reluctance to be publicly credentialed for a contribution not really motivated by the desire for public acclaim. Whenever the Queen came on TV he would stand up and he would get very, very upset if anyone made the remotest quip. He was very dicey about things like that, there was only Heifetz and The Queen. He was dead set serious about those two.

M: I need to get into his mind through you. Why were you both so accommodating and agreeable to play with us? Neither of you were ever condescending.

B: There were aspects to Dad, which are very similar to his son. It never occurred to me to think any other way but to make great music. There is a parallel here to making a choice. I like to be friends with outcasts, interesting and unusual people. I still have such friends, the ones that didn't fit in, they're often very thoughtful, sensitive people, and sometimes funny looking as well. I remember a friend saying, 'You know, you really shouldn't be seen with this or that person'. It never occurred to me to think that way. I wouldn't say I had pride about it, but I've always been like that, and Dad was similar.

Dad also had friends who were misfits, and he always had a soft spot for them. It wasn't because he felt he was doing them service, it's just that he had a genuine feeling for them.

M: Are you saying that we are all misfits in the Doctors Orchestra?

B: No, no, no, no, no, no, no. Not at all.

The point is, I think it comes from a similar sense where you are looking at the motivation of the people playing. I have turned down some very high-profile engagements because I just don't want to work with this person, I know what they're like. We've all had this experience in different fields. It's got to do with their motivation.

M: You didn't feel that with us?

B: No, never because the motivation of the Doctors Orchestra is so good. It's all about motivation and the only reason someone would hold back would be fearing that it will reflect poorly on them. I don't have those thoughts or feelings. If I had, I probably would have had a totally different career. I would have thought, I must go overseas, I must have this, I must do that. Not in my nature, period. It's not lack ambition, I have ambition, but it's the motivation that counts.

M: Chris was a perfectionist and yet he could accept all the imperfections that an amateur orchestra brings with it. The essence and the feeling of the music was always there so he could forgive our imperfections.

B: He would have thought of it as forgiving. He was quite practical and worked with the materials he had. Sometimes he'd come home after a rehearsal, put on a record and say, 'Oh my God. It's so far from X, Y, and Z.

M: He was fun to work with. He enjoyed our association, and he had a lot of respect for doctors. Deep down, he really enjoyed bossing us around ,as we just had to do what he told us.

B: No question about that, he had a very strong hierarchical respect. It comes from his working- class hard background, that sense of what status people of status had achieved in their lives, that meant a great deal to him. It meant a great deal to be taken out by the 'big' guys.

M: That's funny because we all thought of him as the big guy. I remember he spoke very fondly of a lady who arranged a scholarship for him from a philanthropic trust to the Royal College of Music.

B: That's something I still have to learn from him. He was always very appreciative and thankful to those who helped him.

M: To what extent are the concerts that we have done together significant to you? Do you feel a sense of achievement?

B: The Sydney Town Hall Grieg concert was very special in 1997, playing on that beautiful Italian made Fazioli.

M: I flew up to check which pianos were available. They had a Steinway Grand and a Fazioli. When I mentioned that to Chris, he went off his head that you MUST have the Steinway. He was always very protective of you.

B: Actually, one of the difficulties I had with Dad, and this is very personal, and not a criticism, but he projected his high standards onto me in a way that wasn't always the best for me. He would often say, 'Oh, Ben wouldn't put up with this or Ben wouldn't accept that.' It was probably subconscious.

M: He lived out a lot of his aspirations through you.

B: That was difficult. But I loved doing the Grieg. I also enjoyed doing the Triple Concerto very much and even the 2001 concert on the baby grand. It's what I call a tractor, not a proper instrument.

M: What was wonderful to see was how you coped performing on that tiny piano. Others with your talent, sophistication and artistry would have chucked a wobbly, but you didn't. There were no histrionics or diva type behaviour. You just said, 'Okay, we'll just get on with it'. But Chris was really put out and upset though.

B: For me, getting outraged would take away from my performance.

There are some artists that actually get a rise, a sort of kick, out of histrionics, it really helps them play better, there were also singers like Birgit Nilsson. Some have sex or they had to do something outrageous just before a performance. Not me.

M: Embarrassing that we couldn't provide you with a proper instrument. I used to fly interstate multiple times to check on things like that in the years of the Grieg and the Triple Concertos. The committee were meeting weekly, but on Zoom, no one physically went there to check on the baby grand. Face to face is always best.

M: What would be your desert island choices?

B: I'm going to be very cliche here. Funnily enough the late Beethoven quartets break me up too much. I'm not sure I could deal with them. I might even want to go for something a little bit more popular, like Caetano Veloso. If I was really on a desert island listening to the slow movement of Beethoven it would crush me. I'd probably want something lighter, it ain't gonna be Shostakovich or Mussorgsky's 'Pictures at an Exhibition' or Rimsky Korsakoff's 'Sheherezade' either. I really can only think of what I would not want to hear.

M: You knew Chris's passion for English music. At our third ever concert which was in Sydney, it was an all Elgar program put together with only three rehearsals. We just made it after Chris cut a few of the more difficult variations of Elgar's 'Enigma'. The Elgar Cello Concerto went well with LiWei as our soloist. I asked Li Wei afterwards what he thought of our orchestra:

'It's as good as any school orchestra I've played with.'

He may even have meant it as a compliment, I'd like to think we're much better than that now.

B: Elgar's 'In the South', it's so uplifting and Dad loved it, an incredible piece.

M: I only hated Chris once, when he made us play 'Job' by Vaughan Williams. I could never get my head around that piece.

B: He really liked that piece and it's not my favourite Vaughan Williams at all. I adore his music but agree that piece is odd. Dad was an enlightened kind of person but there was a strong religious strain in him, no question. He gravitated towards the biblical narrative because the Old and New Testament parables are incredibly powerful. I remember opening his door, he was really in tears. He was listening to Bach's St. Matthew Passion with Peter Piers. Those things went very deep with him, the music and the whole narrative which is so overwhelming. Doesn't matter if you consider yourself religious or not as Hartmut (Lindemann, Violist) said, 'I am religious when I hear Bach'.

There was a religious attitude, in Dad.

M: His parents were Salvation Army, weren't they?

B: Yes, there was that sense of the sacred aspect of life. There was a religious depth to him. Job had something of that narrative but it's not one of his most wonderful pieces of music.

M: He embraced your mother's Jewishness and had a great respect for Jews.

B: He was an honorary Jew really. The story of Job deeply affected him. Constant punishment and still having faith, that story really stirred him.

M: I never knew that religious side of him, but he was an incredibly generous and ethical person. Chris told me walking across a park at night in East Melbourne when a beggar stopped him. 'Have you got a dollar mate?'

'Geez, I'm sorry, mate, I've only got a $50 note.'

'Oh, don't worry about it then mate', then they both walked on.

An amazingly trusting thing to do in the middle of the park at night.

B: He was no angel, he could be brutal: a complex man, but a very beautiful heart.

He had this extraordinary quality. There are people that are just loved and there are people that are respected, then there are people that are feared. Dad needed to be loved, and he was loved.

Personally, I know I'm respected and I think I'm liked, but to be loved like dad, that's a gift. And he was loved, wasn't it?

M: Absolutely, but he loved people too, that's why he was loved back.

B: Maybe he felt he was loved at the expense of being respected, and I think that's why he gravitated to me in a way. I don't have the need to be liked. You knew him well enough to know that he did not want to deal with any hostility.

No one wants to be disliked, but it was a big thing for him. At the same time, he wanted to be respected. When you're so loved, people over-relate. Respect is a sort of distance, isn't it, but there was no distance with Dad, it just wasn't there. That impinged on his sense of security because he reacted, 'Who do you think you are?'

M: He never finished his degree at the Royal Academy of Music because he had excellent opportunities to join well established quartets and chamber orchestras without it. He told me whenever the music faculty met at the University of Melbourne he was always addressed as Mr. Martin instead of professor or associate professor. I don't think it bothered him particularly.

B: Off the record, I didn't really complete anything either. I went to Julliard, and I didn't do badly, but I can't really boast about credentials. I followed a bit in the same line, I advanced by getting my hands dirty.

For a musician the credentials are how you play and who you play with. You're good as your last concert.

M: What does music mean to you?

B: I can say what a piano means to me. Piano is my sanity. The sheer tactile relationship and contact with an instrument where you are creating something physical in terms of airwaves and sound. Akin to being a carpenter. If I didn't have the piano, I'd get it all in my head and probably lose all perspective. I think in a musical way, instinctively. Every aspect of musical notation is hardwired into me. Even the actual notational system has been a source of deep fascination for me with all its inherent flaws. I have a natural obsession with it, it's also a conceptual obsession. I was reading, Leo Tolstoy's, 'What is art?' recently. He had a pretty disparaging view. He felt Beethoven in his later compositions had lost the general public. Tolstoy felt Beethoven had become too intellectual. He felt music was for the every man and I feel a bit like that too. I am like Dad, I love a good tune,

I'll always love a good tune, we shared that. Samuel Barber, the American composer, when asked about a contemporary piece he had just heard said,

'Wouldn't have minded a good tune'.

Whatever the kind of music I write, I know how difficult it is to write a good tune. I don't think music is this universal language but that's a very big subject. I don't even know if it's a language. Let's just talk about the great composers. I was wanting to get an interview happening with music, just for musicians to say, why is art important? Why is it valuable? Because these great writers access something that we can't access within ourselves? Schubert can stare into that void much longer than most of us, Chopin the same. And without being terrified by it, they draw something out and make it beautiful. There's no question. It is also true of literature, Dante's 'Inferno', Goethe's 'Faust' or Milton's 'Paradise Lost'.

They are depicting the grand horror, which is hell, but they make it palatable so that we can bear to think about what would otherwise terrify the be Jesus out of us. That's why I get upset when people talk about non-essentials. If you take away all that you're taking away the connection that people have with the sense of the unknown that they can touch, and they're not terrified. Music is depicting often the horrors but bringing them to us in a palatable way which we actually enjoy. We enjoy the ride with the devil. Horowitz the great pianist, knew how to ride with the devil, as did the great writers. These are ways of us keeping in touch with the unknown, things that would otherwise frighten us.

M: Do you feel you have to play every day?

B: I like to touch the piano every day. Busoni, famously said, 'You should get to the piano every day, it's very nice.' Medtner said, 'you should compose everyday'. I don't manage that, but I do get to the piano every day. Just the contact with the piano is therapeutic.

M: How old were you when you first felt this strong affinity for the piano?

B: Probably when I began lessons aged 7.

M: Was it your idea to learn or was it your parent's?

B: I took to it naturally, it was an immediate form of expression, I just loved it.

I wasn't a disciplined practiser at all. Not until I went to Juilliard in America. That's where I really started practising for many, many hours. The Americans are very hard workers. You had to sit in the practice room because you couldn't have dinner with anyone till they finished their practice at 10 o'clock in the evening.

Dr Chris Hughes
MBBS, FRANZCOG

Obstetrician Gynaecologist, Double Bass

'The romance of a little moment of beautiful music is everywhere'

What was your earliest musical experience?

My earliest childhood memories were of music in the house. I started playing the piano when I was in primary school. My mother played. I remember lying in bed on hot summer nights unable to sleep with mum playing Debussy; the music wafting up the passageway. I pestered her to let me learn and I ended up having lessons with the man who had taught her. Mr. George Findlay, who was blind. He taught at the school for the blind and in the vestry in a church in Glen Iris.

I went to a secondary school at Scotch College where there was a strong music program and all students were introduced to trying out flute, violin and cello or bass. Like so many things in life, we are influenced by a charismatic person who becomes our mentor and that leads us into whatever field or instrument we chose. We had a lovely old rogue at school who taught double bass called Tom Howley. Tom had grown up the son of a country doctor and he had played for a long time with the MSO. He had wonderful stories of the old days with the orchestra, including playing with Stravinsky who he described conducting 4 beats with one hand and 5 with the other

I took lessons with Tom right through secondary school and beyond. I did bass as a year 12 subject. The school had an orchestral program which included an overseas tour when I was in year 11. It was my first time on an aeroplane, and we went to Singapore, Kuala Lumpur and Bangkok. It was a really rewarding experience and several people from that orchestra ended up becoming professional musicians.

Can you remember a time when music first spoke to you?

I remember hearing various bits of classical and pop music. There's something hardwired in my brain so that you can play me a pop song from the early or mid-1960's and I could sing along with it even if I couldn't actively remember the lyrics.

What was your most exciting musical experience as a listener and as a player?

Susan and I were on holiday while we were living in England. We went to Paris and chanced upon a recital concert in the old Paris Opera given by Joan Sutherland. Her accompanist was her husband, Richard Bonynge. She wore an outrageous big grey tulle skirt that stretched outwards forever with acres and acres of fabric. A rainbow of coloured sequins stretched across the full length of the dress.

The audience was mesmerised by her and after about 45 encores she sang 'There's no place like home'. It was very simple and absolutely beautiful.

I had a friend at university who had muscular dystrophy and was confined to an electric wheelchair. He was the student union welfare officer. Staying with him as his overnight carer was rewarding because I got some insight into people who live with disability. He was a wonderful rogue and a fun person to be with. After living with him for a couple of months we had become very good friends.

Music Is Medicine

He was an activist for 'wheelchair access reform' in public buildings. He would make a point of gaining access looking as awkward as possible so people would notice.

At a cinema in the CBD, I would park the car and get out his electric wheelchair. It was a great heavy thing. I'd assemble it at the top of the stairs that we were about to negotiate. Then I would carry him up the stairs and plonk him in the wheelchair. In order to carry him he would put his arms around me, and I would hug him. The scene was of two men hugging with his limp legs dangling in the breeze. We would get some very quizzical looks and I would sing a version of that old song "he ain't heavy he's my brother". But I'd sing he is heavy and he's not my brother.

As an act of gratitude for living with him he gave me a couple of tickets to hear Lenny Bernstein and the New York Philharmonic who were on tour in Melbourne. The concert was in the Melbourne Town Hall. We sat near the front, and they played a Tchaikovsky Symphony. I remember this wonderful gesture from Bernstein as he opened his hand to shape a note from the French horn. It was as if he just placed the note in the air and the note exploded. A moment of sheer magic.

I get a bit schmaltzy about things at times and it's not necessarily dependent on the quality of the band. It's happened a bit when playing Tchaikovsky. You're sitting in this huge music-making machine that's building up to a romantic climax. I say to myself, bite your lower lip, just stop yourself crying. I'm an absolute sucker for that kind of thing.

I remember going down to string school with Michael Fortescue and Christian Wojtowycz. Sedivka was another of those charismatic figures. We played the Albinoni Adagio with a large string orchestra. That was a moment and a half.

I took a year off Medicine and played in a couple of shows including Jesus Chris Superstar. I was undecided whether to try to be a musician or a medico. I taught a few students and played in the Victorian

College of the Arts Orchestra, (VCA). During that year I got a locum playing with the Elizabethan Trust Orchestra for a month, the best band I had ever played with.

We were rehearsing a Beethoven Symphony, I was thinking, oh God, this is just so great, the orchestra is sounding so good. Then people started to cough and clear their throats repeatedly. What was going on? Various people stopped playing and continued coughing and clearing their throats. I couldn't work out what was happening. Then one of the players said, 'Excuse me Maestro, it's a designated union tea break.'

I was shocked and disillusioned; I was so immersed in the music and the sound. And then to stop all of a sudden, I realised that for all these people, this was just another day at work. It was tea-break and they all downed tools. It was a moment of realisation. I was never going to be a hot shot soloist or anything but that killed the romance of music as a career for me.

A couple of the professionals who played with us regularly in Corpus Medicorum have mentioned that there's a feeling that, although played by amateurs, this is the best kind of music making with everyone motivated and wanting to be there.

What does music mean to you?

I don't have an easy answer, but Covid has demonstrated what the absence of music is.

I love having music around. I often listen to ABC classic FM which is on in the background, but I'm not bound up in that daily. Music is part of the rhythm of life as I get older. I like looking at trees and walking on the beach. The romance of a little moment of beautiful music is everywhere. I don't have a name to give to that process.

Can you remember a time when things went wrong in a performance?

We've had a couple of times in recent years where we've been planning to repeat passages in the score and when we reached that point, we were not sure whether to repeat or not? A shared terrible empty feeling goes around the orchestra. It's the same thing that I've felt a few times, right at the beginning of an operation. I know exactly what to do but in an odd moment of reflection, 'Ooh hang on how do I do this?' Similarly standing over the golf ball about to drive, you think, 'Oh, hang on, how do you hit a golf ball again?'

What are your desert island choices?

I was just listening to that very radio program on the BBC. It was an interview with Charlie Watts the drummer in the 'Stones' who recently died. He was an interesting sort of a cat. Charlie Watts chose some Shostakovich, Fred Astaire, Frank Sinatra and a bit of jazz. For me, one of the movements from the Bach cello suites, the Sarabande from the fifth suite, is sad and beautiful.

How much do you practise?

I practise in a sawtooth kind of way; I practise a lot in preparation for a concert and then I lapse. With the lockdown I've had this mentality, 'just get through this, it's just for a couple of weeks.' Now that they've made the announcement about prolonged lockdown, I feel, 'hang on, just stop wasting your life, get on and do a few things like some structured practice.'

As I mentioned earlier, I had a year off medicine when I toyed with the idea of being a professional musician. However, I had decided to go back and do medicine. I got a telephone call from the Dean's secretary of the VCA, John Hopkins to go to his office. I walked in and he said, 'Why haven't I received an application from you for next year?' It was an awkward moment because he was a member of one of those religious sects who were unsympathetic to conventional medicine. I think it was something of an affront to him that I had decided to return to medicine.

My music fell away to pretty well nothing. Then someone invited me to play with the Australian Doctors Orchestra. I can't remember who it was exactly, but I joined the second ADO concert. Although I've missed a few I've played in many over the years. It's been a lovely, lovely experience, a n d I feel a lifetime indebtedness to you, ,Miki for having initiated that. I truly do, it's been a wonderful thing. I remember early on in the orchestra; you sent me a little framed photograph of a article from 'Surgical News' that had a picture of people in the orchestra. You'd written a personal note on the back, I was just really touched by that.

It's been such a lovely thing to be able to participate in playing at a good level as well as enjoying the social side of it without it being my career. I've had the same 150-year-old instrument all my adult life. After some damage Ben Puglisi rebuilt it. He dismantled it completely, reset the belly to repair cracks and then put it together again. He inserted a couple of carbon fibre rods to reinforce the neck as well as various other things over the years. It's a bit like grandpa's axe but has been my lifelong companion.

Dr Stuart Paige

MBBS, FANZCA, AFRACMA

Anaesthetist, Bass Trombone

'I can't remember a performance when things didn't go wrong... so, if you're not confident shut up. I've had to shut up a few times....as you know.'

Stuart is best described as one of our cheeriest, most enthusiastic, and funniest members of ADO. There, right at the beginning, he reminded me that though he was registered for the premier concert as Bass Trombonist in 1993 he never got to play as there were no Bass Trombones required at that concert. I wonder if he ever got a refund. Knowing Stuie, he wouldn't care. The Bass Trombone situation was quickly remedied, and subsequent concerts were programmed to enable all sections of the orchestra to be able to participate.

What was your earliest musical recollection?

My father was a professional musician, (trumpet player) and I grew up in a house with a lot of music, mostly classical, but some jazz, and quite a bit of brass band. This formed a lot of my early memories.

Did you have a fascination for brass because of that?

Yes, I think so. Actually I had a bit of a fascination with the trumpet, but I managed to have a fight with a little dog when I was a kid and the dog won, so I had quite a nasty scar in the middle of my top lip. I had to pick an instrument with a larger mouthpiece, so I headed for the trombone.

Which was your first ADO?

I was fully paid up and registered for the first one, but the concert didn't include brass. I have been in all the major concerts since then.

What has ADO has given you, what do you think about ADO?

A marvelous sense of camaraderie and a continuation of my interest in classical music. It's really been at the forefront of maintaining my enthusiasm for music.

Do you play with other groups in Toowoomba or Brisbane?

Yes, I've played a few times with the Queensland Medical Orchestra as well as brass and jazz bands here in Toowoomba. As you know I have also played several times and with the European Doctors Orchestra and the World Doctors Orchestra. They have all been great experiences. I have also very much enjoyed my performances with Corpus Medicorum (Victorian Doctors Orchestra).

I remember you flew over to join us for the premiere concert with the European Doctors orchestra at your own cost.

Yes, I must admit I don't have many hobbies so a really good bass trombone and an airfare isn't as much as a Stradivarius. I tell my wife she has saved a lot of money by maintaining an interest in a bass trombonist.

Do you remember when music first spoke to you?

Yes, I do. This sounds a little old fashioned, but my father subscribed to Readers Digest Music, a large LP compilation of classical music and he often played three or four pieces from that collection. They included Von Suppé's Light Cavalry Overture, Dvorak's New World Symphony and Elgar's Pomp and Circumstance March. He could play Richard Strauss's first horn concerto part from memory. It took him a lot of practice and I still remember every note. These were great childhood memories, I was about 8 or 9 at the time.

What was the most exciting music you have experienced both as a player and listener?

That's easy. I've been enchanted with this piece of music for over 20 years, it's Scheherazade, by Rimsky-Korsakoff. We played it in Hobart with ADO in 2019, it is just a fantastic piece of music.

And as a listener?

The symphony I enjoy most is Mahler 5. The slow movement is fantastic. Leonard Bernstein conducted it for Robert Kennedy's funeral. Incredibly moving.

How many hours a week do you spend playing your instrument, especially now that you are retired?

My wife just called out "too many". They can be cruel. I practise every day for at least three quarters of an hour, maybe a little more. Two nights a week we have band rehearsal for 3 hours. We give seven or eight performances a year, but of course that's been less this last year because of COVID.

What does music mean to you?

It's really my major interest outside of family life. We have grandchildren and people we run around with. They all keep us busy. We go up to the North Coast a bit for relaxation, but music is everything to me outside family stuff.

Can you remember a performance when things went wrong?

I can't remember a performance when things didn't go wrong. I learned from a fantastic first trumpet player, (Jeff Spiller) who was a member of the Queensland Symphony Orchestra. Tutoring us, he told us that by far the best mistakes a brass player can make are silent ones. So, if you're not confident shut up.

I have had to shut up a few times. I can't remember too many sour notes in the orchestra. As you know, I'm not too great at rhythm and I'm working on that. I have certainly missed a few entrances. I don't know if you remember when I went over to play with you in EDO and we were playing one of Elgar's Pomp and Circumstance marches, which had a very high note for bass trombone, so I bought a special mouthpiece and practised this note a hundred times a day, in my hotel room and at your place. At the performance, when it came for me to play, I was concentrating so hard and counting that I counted straight through the entry and I never did get to play that note (lots of laughter). A mouthpiece cost a couple of hundred bucks.

What is the question you least want me to ask you.

I am thinking of retiring from music because I'm getting too old. I think it is true that your ability to cope with necessary hand-eye coordination issues, and sudden changes in rhythm and your wind capacity, especially for trombone players, becomes more of a problem as you get older, but I'm going to hang in there for a little while yet.

What are your Desert Island, choices?

From a purely trombone point of view, I would take as much Urbie Green as I could. Fantastic sound, beautiful mellow tone. From a trumpet point of view, I would take Rafael Mendez, and then perhaps, Scheherezade, Brahms's first Symphony and Mahler's fifth.

Well, you've got a very eclectic taste.

Yeah, I guess.

Is there anything else you would like to add?

I wish to emphasise how important ADO and music in general are to me. ADO has been a central part of my life for nearly 30. We have both made great friends and had a lot of fun.

I might conclude with a couple of examples of 'fun'.

We were playing in Adelaide, with Chris Martin conducting ADO, he wanted the bass drum to be played very softly, like distant thunder. This was at rehearsal and the bass drummer couldn't hear Chris, so he asked me what he had said. Naturally I replied that Chris wanted him to hit the bloody thing. Eight bars later this bloke powered into the drum. Chris went very pale. I have never been asked for advice since.

You remember after an EDO concert when we were in a lift in London with Larry from Rumania going up to your apartment. The lift was very small, and Larry is a giant of a man (but lovely). As it happens, I was pushed into his chest. I came up to the middle of his shirt and without thinking said, 'a hundred and forty'. He dropped his upper lip like a naughty kid and said, 'a hundred and forty- two'. I was ashamed that I had inadvertently embarrassed him, but we all had a good laugh later.

Jeffrey V. Rosenfeld AC, OBE, KStJ

MB BS(Melb), MD(Monash), MS(Melb),
FTSE, FAHMS, FRACS, FRCS(Edin),
FACS, IFAANS,
FRCS(Glasg) Hon, FRCNST Hon,
FRCST Hon, GradDipMusPerf(Melb),
LMusA, RAAMC

Emeritus Professor, Department of Surgery, Monash University,
Senior Neurosurgeon, The Alfred Hospital
Adjunct Professor in Surgery, F. Edward Hébert School of Medicine,
Uniformed Services University of the Health Sciences, Bethesda, Maryland, USA Clinical Professor (Honorary), Dept. Surgery, Chinese University of Hong Kong
Adjunct Professor (Research), Department of Electrical and Computer Systems Engineering, Monash University
Professor (Honorary), Department of Surgery, University of Papua New Guinea
Major General (Ret'd), Australian Defence Force

Neurosurgeon, Clarinet

INTRODUCTION

Jeffrey was given a recorder at school, when he was 5 years old and ever since, he has been obsessed with the woodwind family of instruments. His main love, however, is the clarinet. As a string player, I was unaware of the subtle evolution of the clarinet because the violin has changed little in 400 years. At the end of our interview, I added a pictorial clarinet addendum for clarification. Currently, Jeffrey is studying the five-key period clarinet ,which was played in the mid-eighteenth century.

On being asked what music means to him:

'It is a privilege to operate on the human brain, to remove a tumour or a vascular malformation and cure the patient. It is an exacting technical challenge requiring judgement and skill but there is also an art and beauty to brain surgery. This art and beauty are quite different from the beauty and power of music to profoundly move my soul. Yes, looking at and touching the living brain is a beautiful experience, but this is not like the ecstasy or pathos I experience when listening to the best music.'

It's not every day that I get to interview a neurosurgeon, professor, clarinetist, Major General, and a Knight, simultaneously, in the one man. How are you coping with lockdown inflicted on us again?

With lockdown, I'm just at home, having Zoom meetings and working on my Master of Music thesis and practising. I am also learning a new instrument, the Period (or Classical) Clarinet which is totally different from the modern clarinet.

Is that the same as a basset horn?

No, you're thinking of the basset clarinet. I've actually ordered a basset clarinet, but it hasn't arrived yet. I will put the basset clarinet in context.

The five-key clarinet was the standard clarinet used in the second half of the eighteenth century. The basset clarinet was a special clarinet that was developed for Anton Stadler, Mozart's favourite clarinetist, and he wrote a number of pieces for it. The clarinet concerto and the clarinet quintet are the best known. Mozart's opera 'La Clemenza di Tito' also has a wonderful aria, 'Parto parto' in which the basset clarinet has an exciting duet with the mezzo-soprano, Sesto. There are not many pieces for the basset clarinet, but it has a beautiful sound. There is wonderful ABC recording of my teacher, Craig Hill playing the Mozart clarinet concerto on the basset clarinet which is well worth listening to. Surprisingly, there is only one drawing of it in existence. Anton Stadler asked his instrument maker to add some extra keys and length to the instrument so as to extend the range down to C below the bottom E on the standard clarinet.

The basset horn is a different instrument. It is an alto clarinet which has a shape like a saxophone and was used by Mozart in his requiem and 'Gran Partita'. . The earliest clarinets had only two keys but many holes of course. By contrast, the modern clarinet has seventeen keys which are joined together in a system called the French Boehm system or the German Öehler system. By adding these keys, the clarinet could play smoothly and accurately in all keys.

What were your earliest musical recollections?

I was given a recorder as a five-year-old and I used to play it in class. We had group singing, and we learned to read music. At Gardiner Central School Mrs. Stanley was our music teacher in primary school. During singing, I was playing the recorder and accompanying the rest of the class, with Mrs. Stanley playing the piano. At school concerts I played the recorder and the clarinet. I still love playing the recorder. I used to play continuously in my parents' car while we were driving around in our old black FJ Holden. The radio was on and I would accompany whatever was playing, pop, classical, anything, I just couldn't put the recorder down. I had an obsession with music from a young age.

I am now a serious player of the baroque recorder which has a lower pitch than the modern recorder (A=415Hz). Handel and Telemann were prominent amongst many baroque composers who wrote beautiful music for the recorder.

It's a craft to make the recorder sound good.

I have a beautiful baroque recorder and another one at concert pitch, made by Joanne Saunders, a Melbourne maker. She was apprenticed to Frederick Morgan. He was the doyen of recorder makers internationally. Great recorder players from around the world played Morgan recorders. His instruments are now collectors' items. He was making them in country Victoria. He was the Stradivarius of the recorder makers. They sounded gorgeous. Joanne has now become one of the best recorder makers in the world.

Describe your musical journey with the clarinet?

When I was eight, I started to learn the clarinet and saxophone from a jazz musician Harry James. In secondary school, I learnt clarinet from Phillip Miechel, who was the principal clarinettist in the Melbourne Symphony Orchestra (MSO). It was fantastic to be able to learn from a world-class player.

Later in high school I played in the school orchestra conducted by that great music teacher Bruce Worland. I also learnt the oboe, bassoon and flute and learnt to play jazz with a pianist called Brian Martin. I also played the French horn whilst at university.

I did well in VCE clarinet and got into the Australian Youth Orchestra (AYO) in 1971. I missed the AYO tour to China but went on the Queensland tour (laughter). We played in Brisbane and Toowoomba. Jeffrey Crellin was in AYO at the same time as me, and he became principal oboe in the MSO for many years. We keep in touch.

I got into medicine at that stage, but I had a dilemma deciding whether I should do medicine or music, I kept music as my recreation and hobby, and medicine as my career. Now that I've retired from clinical practice, I am reversing the order and music has become predominant. Family of course comes before both. During medical school I used to regularly play in dance bands and jazz groups all over town.

I was fortunate to have lessons from the leading clarinettist, Paul Dean when he was Director of the Australian National Academy of Music and then from Justin Beere, Associate Principal Clarinet in Orchestra Victoria. So, you can see I've had the privilege of learning from the best clarinettists. I put on a dream of a birthday concert at ANAM in 2012 which involved Paul Dean and Jeffrey Crellin. I'll never forget our performance of the Mozart 'Gran Partita' for thirteen wind instruments.

I did the AMEB Licentiate exam which was quite challenging. Amongst the works I played was the Gerald Finzi clarinet concerto which is a gorgeous work which deserves to be better known. I completed my Graduate Diploma of Music in 2020, which was a very big undertaking because it compresses a three year Bachelor of music degree into one year. I learnt a lot, including conducting, baroque performance, music history, harmony, counterpoint, clarinet performance and chamber music.

MJP and JR Thailand Surgical meeting

I am now doing a Master of Music degree by research (Performance) at the University of Melbourne Conservatorium, concentrating on performance of eighteenth century clarinet works on five- and six-key clarinets. I am really enjoying discovering new things about this music and the evolution of the clarinet. I am so fortunate to be learning from the period clarinet specialist Craig Hill who also plays in the MSO.

How did you manage with Covid lockdowns?

A lot of the lessons were on Zoom. I was having weekly lessons with David Griffiths, the head of clarinet studies at the Melbourne Conservatorium. One of the students would play a solo piece in woodwind classes and we'd all listen, but it's not the same as being together face-to-face in a room.

Was there much music in your home as a child?

We had gramophone records, my parents played Italian and American popular music. From my interest in the recorder my parents wondered what instrument I should learn. They liked the sound of the clarinet after hearing Woody Herman, Artie Shaw and Benny Goodman.

Can you remember when music first spoke to you?

I was four or five and we used to go to my grandparents' place every week. They had a 78- gramophone player. The record collection included popular music, jazz and classical. During our visits I would play the records and sing along.

A piece that especially sticks with me, was 'Moonlight Serenade', played by Glenn Miller's orchestra. It's beautiful music and resonated with me. It has lovely clarinet solos throughout, playing the melody accompanied by saxophones and brass. That was one of the first pieces of music that I fell in love with, believe it or not.

What was your most exciting musical experience first as a player and then as a listener?

Playing in the Australian Youth Orchestra was unforgettable. Corpus Medicorum and the Australian Doctors Orchestra playing gorgeous music is also a real joy and privilege. I can't single out any particular piece, there were so many memorable moments.

Jeffrey V. Rosenfeld AC, OBE, KStJ

In terms of listening, I have a broad taste ranging from renaissance to far edge modern jazz and some pop. I particularly love high baroque, Bach and Handel. The oboe obligatos in Bach's choral works are achingly beautiful. I love all Mozart, but the late Mozart piano concertos are especially gorgeous pieces of music, and of course Beethoven and Brahms symphonies and piano concertos. I love Mozart operas; I could listen to them all day. I was just listening to 'Magic Flute' yesterday. These are pieces that I keep coming back to, not to mention Mozart's clarinet concerto and quintet, I love playing and listening to them. I also love the operas of Handel, Verdi, Puccini, Bellini and Donizetti. For me, Maria Callas singing 'Casta Diva' or 'Vissi d'Arte' is the pinnacle of human emotional expression in song.

What, what does music mean to you?

Music is, an essential part of my life, I find music is able to penetrate my soul and influence the way I feel and think. It influences my perception of sound and emotion, it can bring me to tears, and it can bring me joy and happiness. You can read a good book and it's very meaningful and enjoyable, you can look at a great painting and enjoy the colours and skill of the artists, but music is just something beyond that, it reaches into the deeper recesses of the mind and soul. It is something that is very powerful in my life.

It is a privilege to operate on the human brain, to remove a tumour or a vascular malformation and cure the patient. It is an exacting technical challenge requiring judgement and skill but there is also an art and beauty to brain surgery. This art and beauty is quite different from the beauty and power of music to profoundly move my soul. Yes, looking at and touching the living brain moves my emotions, but this is not like the ecstasy or pathos I experience when listening to the best music.

Can you remember things going wrong in a performance?

I was playing in the Sibelius violin concerto a couple of years ago and was unnecessarily very nervous because there was an exposed clarinet part. A short clarinet solo comes in after eight bars. The violin starts and then comes the clarinet part which seems totally out of place. Despite the conductor cueing me in I lost my count and missed my entry. The conductor was getting agitated and kept waving his arms, luckily very few would have noticed because musically it's not that important. The clarinet is frequently very exposed in a symphony orchestra and playing it is like walking a tightrope. It's very easy to fall off. You have to control your nerves as you would in surgery

Isn't it interesting that we don't get anxious while operating but we do in live performance.

The best neurosurgeons have a calmness about them, they have a logical sequence of steps they follow and are very efficient in their movements, ergonomically speaking. They plan several moves ahead. They will rehearse the operation in their mind before they actually do it. They anticipate problems. You can do that more efficiently with experience, but essentially, the key to being a fine surgeon is to be compassionate to the patient but cold and calculating in the surgical planning, very determined in action but very smooth and delicate in the execution. I try to transpose that calmness in my surgery to playing in an orchestra.

If you're anxious and get a bit of a tremor, your hand will shake, and you will make mistakes because you're not thinking straight. You're thinking about the wrong things and it's exactly the same thing that happens with music, you're not in the right frame of mind.

Playing a clarinet solo that everyone is listening to is very exposed. There are many ways you can play it, loud, soft, fast, slow, and also articulate it in a number of ways. There are many aspects to think about, and you've planned and practised it over and over; you know what and how you want to play it, but even then, it may not come out the way you had planned.

Happily, the repercussions are not as severe as when you're doing neurosurgery.

Correct. That's the thing that you have to realise, the stress of neurosurgery at the highest level can be almost too much to bear. You've got someone's life in your hands, or you could damage someone just by moving a millimetre either side of the planned surgery or interfering with a tiny blood vessel. At worst, they could lose their life. Again, it's walking the tightrope. If you fall, the patient will fall with you. It's very stressful, but you learn to handle the stress, stay calm and clear-minded.

There is also tension and stress playing in an orchestra, but lives and wellbeing are not at stake. All the same, if you 'stuff-up' you feel as though you've let everyone down around you.

Playing to a big audience doesn't faze me because I've learned to handle the stress. Yes, I still get pre-performance nerves, but not usually to the detriment of my playing.

ADO's premiere performance was in 1993. Can you share your memories of that concert held in Melba Hall.

There were already many doctors playing independently and in small groups. ADO enabled us to come together as a symphony orchestra. It provided a unique opportunity to play beautiful music with good conductors. There are many players in the orchestra who are very fine musicians and the standards we reached were usually pretty high. There were some players who were not that experienced and there were some rough edges around the music, but the key elements of the music were there, and communicated to the audience. We had a fantastic experience making music together.

Do you play every day?

Yes, I do at least an hour of practice every day. I am preparing a seventy minute public recital for my Master of Music degree, so I have to keep up my playing to be able to do that and also of course to play in Corpus Medicorum and ADO.

You're playing mainly a clarinet so when do you get to play those beautiful recorders?

We have a weekly performance class at the Conservatorium. I have been playing the baroque oboe and treble recorder with harpsichord in these classes. Next semester, I'm going to start playing my period clarinet as that's my main objective. I am playing five- and six key-clarinets with forte-piano accompaniment. The pitch of these instruments is at 430 Hz rather than 440 Hz.

Isn't the embouchure quite different from oboe to clarinet?

Yes, very different. My clarinet teacher says I shouldn't play the oboe because it messes up my playing the clarinet, also the fingerings are quite different between the two instruments. I love both instruments so much that I can't help playing them both.

Do your children play any instruments?

I have three children and I used to take them to Suzuki string classes every week. Of the three, only my son Alexander is still playing the violin. You can't force them to play music, you can only show them the way.

Jeffrey V. Rosenfeld AC, OBE, KStJ

You didn't encourage them to play a wind instrument?

It's hard to learn a wind instrument when you're only five or six and I would have loved to have had a string trio so I could play with them. There are some lovely clarinet quartets (Clarinet with three stringed instruments). At least they can read music, understand, and appreciate it.

How demanding is doing a Graduate Diploma of Music in Performance?

It's onerous, it's full time and really demanding. You're doing a lot of subjects at once. There is not much time to do anything else. Going back to university as a student is challenging for an 'old guy' like me. It is hard to do yet more exams, and even more challenging to make recordings of myself playing and conducting to submit for assessment. It's very different from being a consultant neurosurgeon, but very worthwhile because it gave me insight into what I'd  been trying to do for many years, but I didn't really have a detailed understanding of what I was doing. Now I have a much better grasp of the fundamentals, including the history of music and harmony and counterpoint.

While studying baroque performance last year I got to appreciate the baroque style of playing and now I understand how to apply the ornamentation. I have a much deeper understanding of Historically Informed (or Inspired) Performance (HIP).

You also had an army career, and you are a Major General. I believe you've written a textbook of neurosurgery for the Pacific. Is that right?

In my military surgical career, I started as a captain in the army reserve in 1984. I worked my way up through the ranks and eventually became the Surgeon General of the Australian Defence Force (Reserves) and was promoted to Major General which is the highest rank you can attain as a medical officer. I am now retired from the Army.

The book, called 'Neurosurgery in the Tropics' was written for general surgeons and young neurosurgeons so they could diagnose neurosurgical problems and perform neurosurgery in low and middle income countries where there are limited resources.

Have you had many tours of duty overseas?

I've done a lot of civilian volunteer work particularly in Papua New Guinea and Fiji.

How long do you go?

Usually two weeks at a time. I usually go by myself not with a team. I work with the locals surgeons and use their equipment.

Is the army involved with these programmes?

No, that's with the Royal Australasian College's (RACS) global health initiative. I've done eight deployments with the military and because I was trained in general surgery before neurosurgery, all but two of my deployments I worked as a military general surgeon. I went to Rwanda, East Timor twice and to Bougainville twice. I also was deployed to the Solomon Islands and then to Iraq as a neurosurgeon in 2005 and 2017. I was there during the battle of Fallujah and the battle of Mosul.

They were very high intensity battles, resulting in many seriously injured casualties.

What sort of injuries were you dealing with?

As a general surgeon I treated people with problems such as land-mine injuries, a variety of penetrating and blunt trauma, burns, amputations, laparotomies etc. I also had to operate on women with obstetric and gynaecological problems including caesarian sections, emergency hysterectomies for severe postpartum haemorrhage and retained placenta.

In Iraq, I treated many blast and penetrating injuries and this enabled me to become an international expert on blast injury to the head and neck. I've given many lectures and authored many book chapters and articles on these topics. I am a member of an expert panel of the Brain Trauma Foundation which will produce new international guidelines for the management of penetrating head injury.

Will you write your story?

I haven't yet but it's in my head. I will eventually write an autobiography because I've got a lot of interesting tales and experiences to share.

2 Key Clarinet / 1700

Modern day Clarinet, 17 keys

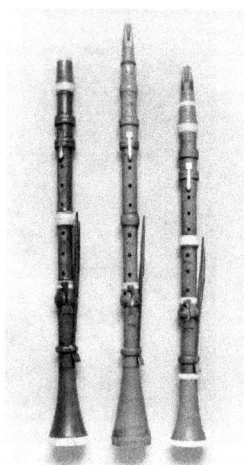

5 Key Clarinet

Basset Horn

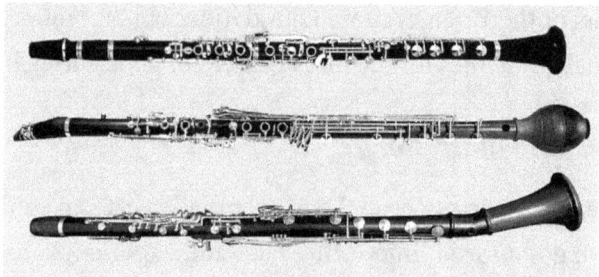

Basset Clarinet

The Joy of the Amateur

Amateur: definition
'Amateur comes from amatore, Latin for lover. It means someone who does something for the love of it rather than money'

*Christopher Martin,
ADO Founding Conductor*

I remember a BBC program where the topic was the joy in pursuit of a number of skills, not necessarily of a exceedingly high standard but at a level that was enjoyable, both for participants and specifically in my case, audience as well.

I have played in many community (amateur) orchestras, and the standards vary enormously. One of my most moving experiences was hearing a concert performed by the Melbourne U3A Orchestra (University of the Third Age). The orchestra is made up of retired professionals of one sort or another and some past members of the Melbourne Symphony orchestra.

The conductor was my close friend Christopher Martin who helped forge the Australian Doctors Orchestra as its inaugural conductor and was later made Conductor Laureate. When Chris was about to retire, he asked my advice on what he should do.

'You should join Rotary's Probus Club and U3A.'

'What the hell are they?'

Chris joined both Probus and U3A. After a year or so he left Probus 'They are all too old'.

He found out that U3A had an orchestra and at his first rehearsal it had a total of 9 members. He was immediately asked to conduct. To his absolute delight, he knew most of the musicians with whom he had worked with in the Melbourne Symphony Orchestra. Their concerts were held on Thursday mornings in the Hawthorn Town Hall. Despite the fact that it was far from perfect playing, knowing some of the participants augmented the experience. Playing on a regular basis gave them a focus, not only for playing music but also to be able to socialise with like-minded people. Hearing and seeing someone you know in an orchestra is a different experience to hearing the Concertgebouw, for instance. You are listening for and enjoying different aspects of the performance.

Bridie Mee

General Practitioner, Oboist

'It's Self Absorbed but Also About Sharing and the human condition'

What are your earliest musical recollections?

I remember growing up hearing my older sister Michaela practising violin. She was very dedicated, practising for hours late into the night. It was rather repetitive, the same intervals over and over again, I remember trying to block it out with a pillow over my head! I also remember that my mum would host my sister's Eisteddfod recitals at our house. I quite enjoyed the performances, especially when our Old English Sheepdog howled. I sometimes helped my
older brother drag him out from under the piano and into the bathroom.

I started piano at a fairly typical age, maybe 6 or 7, and I was very **not** gifted. One lesson my teacher was so bored by my terrible playing and lack of practice that she fell asleep. I ran home gleefully to tell mum, and she let me quit piano after that. At school I was in the recorder ensemble and enjoyed that much more. Mum tried me with the violin too. I can remember my first (and only) violin lesson upstairs in an attic or something, basically wanting to throw the violin out the window. It just didn't feel right, the vibrations through my body, holding up one arm awkwardly, we were not a good match.

The oboe was different. It started when I overheard my sister's friend Ngaire De Korte (now a Professional oboist) play. I think they were practising for school orchestra. Something about it made me want to play. I can't remember what. I think I was about 7 or 8 when I declared I wanted to play the oboe. I was told "no you're too young", and that I'd pop all the blood vessels in my brain if I started at that age. I thought that was a good challenge.

I finally started the oboe in grade 4. My first teacher was Sue Taylor through PLC (the music program there was great), she worked hard to get me to practise. Somehow, I progressed through the exam levels and had some natural talent.

I broke my finger falling off a horse just before my grade 5 exam. Shortly after that we left for America.

What's the difference between the American and Australian reeds and the different sound quality they make?

There are a lot of technical differences between the two scrapes, and also many opinions about those differences. The Americans say that theirs has a deeper, more resonant tone. The rest of the world uses the European scrape, they also say that theirs has a deeper more resonant tone. The European scrape is basically one big scoop from the middle, whereas the Americans scrape is more complicated and fiddly, with a thin tip for

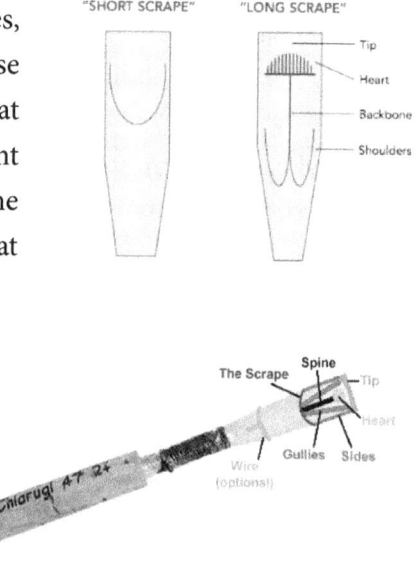

responsiveness (that I'd always accidentally cut off at the corners) and then a thicker part called the plateau to deepen the resonance (which I would take too much out of), then a spine and trenches to create mechanical strength for the reed while allowing the resonance to come through (at least this is how I remember it being explained to me). I used to have a strong opinion but now I can hardly tell the difference when I'm listening.

Do you make your own reeds?

No, I don't make my own reeds now, but reeds have been a big part of my journey with the oboe. For the first few years in Australia, I played on European scrape-reeds made by my teacher Sue. We moved to America when I was 11. I don't remember the change to American scrape being a big deal. A large amount of the weekly oboe lessons were actually spent on reeds, learning how to shape cane, tying them on the tube and whittling the end. I never got very good at it.

I didn't realise at the time how fortunate I was to learn oboe in Cleveland. It is of course the home of the famous Cleveland Orchestra, where John Mack was the principal oboe (from 1965-2001). I took lessons from Dana Sundet, one of his proteges. The style of reed we used required a lot of back pressure and a very strong embouchure, you had to blow rather hard. I saw one of John Mack's reeds once, he'd left it on the stand, it looked like a piece of wood that someone had thrown an axe at. He was pretty blind at that time. It was so thick, but he could make anything play beautifully.

As a teenager I had no idea how lucky I was. I played in the Cleveland Orchestra Youth Orchestra; our rehearsals were in Severance Hall. The principal players from the Cleveland Orchestra took our weekly sectionals. Once a year we had concert where we would sit above the principals, and they'd play second to us. At the time I thought, 'ok cool'. Now it's more like, '**Oh my God that was so amazing**'.

Most of my formative years of playing were in America. I had many amazing opportunities there with youth orchestras, wind ensembles and music camps over the summer, such as Interlochen and Aspen festivals. The summer holidays in the US are three months long, so during high school most parents who can afford it send their kids to "camp".

I got into the undergraduate Cincinnati Conservatory of Music program. I didn't accept the offer though because I suddenly realised becoming a professional oboist would be a terrible idea. I also got into Harvard, and you don't really let that one go. I found out later from someone on my application committee that the oboe recording I sent was the "reason" I got in. I remember thinking, "How hilarious" as I pretty much stopped playing oboe when I got there. I played in the pops orchestra, which was fun, but other than that I didn't play much. The reed making process was really difficult and I found it too stressful. On semester breaks back to Cleveland I'd schedule an oboe lesson just to work on reeds.

At Harvard I majored in the Comparative Study of Religion. I wasn't at all religious but thought I would probably end up working in healthcare where it would be good to have a greater appreciation of religion, and better understand the range of human experience. That degree was basically philosophy of religion, it was a very small and actually very progressive department. To obtain that degree, I had to write a thesis and I needed a challenge because I was thinking of becoming a writer. Although I managed to write the thesis and it was quite good, I realised that I was **not** a natural writer.

After Harvard, I moved back to Australia and tried very hard to avoid going into healthcare (my dad and two siblings were doctors). I still thought I might be a writer or a mounted park ranger to avoid going into health. What was I thinking, I don't even own a horse!

When did music first speak to you?

Honestly..............not until the Australia Doctors Orchestra.

Oh, that's good.

Before then, so much of my music was tied up with the angst of adolescence and perfectionism (a common ailment amongst doctors) so I didn't really enjoy playing. I played because I sounded all right and most my friends were in an orchestra. There was a lot of guilt around that, having talent but no passion, and I found it terribly confusing.

Each concert with the Cleveland Orchestra Youth Orchestra we performed a contemporary piece, and you felt really hard done by if that was the piece assigned to you as first oboe. I was the least dedicated at practising and usually given first oboe on the worst pieces. This one had an incredibly weird atonal solo. I can still remember how I felt playing it some 20 years ago. For some reason I was totally relaxed, and I nailed it. My teacher at the time was Betty Camus, 2nd oboe in the Cleveland Orchestra. After hearing me play she said, 'You could be one of the best oboists in America… but I have no idea why you would want to be'.

So that was the weird burden of having talent, and I know that sounds really privileged but I didn't really enjoy the oboe, and felt very guilty about it. The reality was I could never have become really good because I didn't practice hard enough. It wasn't until I came back to Australia and started playing with ADO that I started enjoying playing again.

After joining ADO I had some lessons with Stephen Robinson and began to understand the complicated layers of my relationship with the oboe. Before ADO I had decided that I was going to quit, mostly because of reeds and the stress of preparing them. But then I made peace with myself and decided to just buy reeds and get someone else to finish them for me. I ordered American reeds to match my oboe, and Stephen made them easier and easier to play with. During one lesson I admitted I just wanted to quit playing all together. To my surprise Stephen said, "No, you can't, it's too important for learning how to deal with anxiety".

It used to be a point of pride in America to have a really hard reed to play. You needed an incredibly strong embouchure to play them. Even as a kid on holidays I took my oboe because if I missed a few days, it could take weeks to get that muscle strength back. This was a completely different approach to Stephen's, which involved playing easier reeds and allowing the sound to come out of you more naturally. Another turning point in my learning from him was realizing that I didn't need to take a big breath before I played, rather I learned to play on empty lungs. The oboe actually doesn't require a lot of air and having emptier lungs makes it less tense.

Another reason I knew I couldn't ever be a professional musician is that I couldn't remember what we played in the last concert.

My first concert with ADO was in Canberra in 2005. I can't remember what we played but everyone was very relaxed and friendly. I'd forgotten to email in any part preferences so was assigned second oboe on one piece. I was just happy to be there. Halfway through rehearsals one of the regular oboists offered to sit out and I could play a bit more. It's just a small example, it's hard to explain, ADO players have such a lovely non-judgmental, inclusive attitude whilst still achieving a rewarding performance standard and that's why I love the ADO so much. I think the balance is absolutely right. Playing and growing with ADO over the last 15 years, I have learnt so much about musical expression and sharing it with other people. It's amazing sitting on a stage with medical musicians, and over the year it's come to feel like family. I haven't had that sense of community in music since being a teenager where I took it for granted and had no idea.

Can you remember your most exciting experiences as a player and as a listener?

Scheherazade! I don't know how I lucked into this, but back in America there was a National Youth Orchestra competition where each orchestra had to send in audition tapes and the top five were chosen. I think all the wind players had to send in their own audition tapes too. The oboist from Chicago had to pull out last minute. I had just auditioned and been accepted by the Cleveland Youth Orchestra, so they called to see if I could fill in.

That's how I ended up playing first oboe in Scheherazade with some absolutely phenomenal young musicians. It was the most amazing experience. I was so sad to miss the 2018 ADO concert in Tasmania with Scheherazade on the program, but I just had a bubba, and it was too soon.

As a listener once again, hearing Sheherezade played by the MSO a couple of years ago. I was up the back sitting on the edge of my seat smiling, I felt like I was floating the whole time, it was amazing to watch.

What does music mean to you?

On the one hand, it's a very self-absorbed experience, but on the other hand it is very much about the human condition, about sharing, sharing yourself, sharing with others and moving into a different place. But it takes a lot of work.

My mother was very dedicated and supported us. She grew up on a sheep farm and apparently begged to play music. Her parents bought her an old piano that was missing half the keys. She never really learned music but she made it a priority for us. Most kids need a lot of help to practice, not many are truly self-motivated. In that sense, Mum gave me classical music. I wish it hadn't been the oboe but that was my own choice!

Playing the oboe is bittersweet in some ways. It's not a relaxing, enjoyable or sexy instrument to play. You do get to play lovely melodies but look constipated while you're playing. And you can't jazz or improvise on the oboe. There's a good reason why there aren't many jazz oboists, it's a terrible idea. I often wish I played the guitar or the saxophone or something.

I was trained in classical music and I am very appreciative, but I feel in some ways that the highest form of music is something like bluegrass or gypsy music as it's more fluid and spontaneous. One of the hardest things for me about Covid is not being able to go and watch live gigs at the local beer garden, not being able to watch my children bopping along enjoying casual music.

Can you remember when things went wrong in a performance?

As an oboist and perfectionist, I can recall almost every mistake I've ever made! But I was playing in one concert as a teenager where we were doing such a terrible job that the conductor just got up and walked away.

What would be your Desert Island, disc choices?

Radio Head is probably my all-time favourite band. Oh, and I do love Beirut. Emma Louise, Sarah Blasko … I'm not really in the habit of listening to much classical, which I always mean to change.

Who were the most significant people that shaped your musical life?

In terms of teachers: Betty Camus. Master classes and sectionals with John Mack. Lessons with John de Lancie at the Aspen music festival. Since moving back to Australia, I've grown a lot musically through lessons with Stephen Robinson. And of course my sister Michaela. It's wonderful having so many shared experiences with her, being able to relate and talk about all the complexities, challenges and joys of both medicine and music.

Is there anything else you want to say about music, the Doctors Orchestra, anything at all before we conclude?

I really can't stress enough how meaningful ADO is to me. It's been quite sad missing concerts in the last 4- 5 years due to having kids and Covid. Hopefully, we can get together and play a concert next year, I'm looking forward to dusting off my oboe.

Osman Ozturk
A. Mus., A, MBBS, FANZCA

Anaesthetist, Violinist Past Concertmaster ADO

'Music is Life, Sun and Oxygen; it's the Cosmos'

What was your earliest music or recollection?

Arthur Rubinstein, playing Chopin on a cassette, I was 9 years old.

There wasn't that much music in the house though Dad was into classical music when he was studying engineering at uni in Ankara, Turkey. He had learnt the violin for a time but didn't pursue it professionally.

Can you remember when music first spoke to you?

When I was a beginner in piano - it was Bach. Little pieces from the book for Anna Magdalena. I just thought: "music is neat". Soon after, I became an avowed Bach-nut and my teacher had difficulty getting me to play anything else! God love her, she was so patient.

Then there were the records in my dad's limited collection. Three come to mind. There was one of Menuhin playing Lalo's "Symphonie Espagnole" with Saint-Saens' "Havanaise" and "Introduction and Rondo Capriccioso" on the other side. Menuhin was seated regally on the cover in a tweed jacket and his famous Stradivarius on the cover, looking as cool as ever.

I listened to that record again and again, practically destroying it.

Another was Arthur Grumiaux playing Paganini's first and fourth concertos. Again, I pretty well wrecked that. There was Grumiaux on the cover, immaculately groomed, like he'd just been to the barber. Such an elegant player, the best!

Finally, there was an album of David Oistrakh playing Bach including the double concerto with his son Igor. That just blew my mind, especially the slow movement of the double concerto.

The piano had already grabbed my imagination, but the violin, that was something else, even when I was only playing on open strings.

My piano teacher was Piroska (Piri) Vojlay, she was so special. She must have sensed my hunger for music. If there was good concert coming up, she would buy an extra ticket and take me with her. We would go to the Franz Liszt Chamber Orchestra, for example. I remember them playing an all- Baroque programme at Dallas Brooks Hall - unthinkable now! Those musicians were amazing.

By far the most formative person in my musical life was Piroska Vojlay. She was all about understanding what music was and learning to love and appreciate it. She took it to another level: she was and is number one, two and three for me.

I came to learn piano almost accidentally. Dad had bought me one of those little Yamaha synthesisers for my ninth birthday. It had a two and a half octave keyboard. Whenever I heard ad jingles on the TV I'd go up to the Yamaha and and pick out the tunes.

Soon after, we moved house and bought an upright piano for 20 bucks from some friends, it was sitting there in their living room as furniture. That piano was with me until I was about 17. It was a tank, made in Chicago by the Cable Company. It sounded like the wild west.

Soon after that, the "Turkish community telegraph" was set in motion. The Consul-General for Turkey in Melbourne heard that I was keen to learn the piano and he said he'd find me a teacher. That's how we found Piri Vojlay. Suddenly I was her pupil, and I was terrified of her.

Music Is Medicine

Hungarians seem to have that effect on people.

Only at first, I loved her very soon afterward. I started with her in 1983 and then by the middle of the next year, she thought I showed promise.

Through her network, she got in touch with the Victorian College of the Arts. I was offered the equivalent of a screen test. I prepared some piano pieces and after I played them the panel asked me to do rhythm and intonation tests. They recommended that I audition for their music high school when the time came. Their policy was that once you graduated, they had to guarantee you employment for a year. As such, they suggested that I should learn an orchestral instrument.

They chose the violin. It was pretty much: 'Learn the violin. Here is the name of a teacher, off you go, see you at the audition.'

Brian Finlayson was my first violin teacher. He had been in Germany for many years and had studied with Igor Ozim. I was with him from 1985 until 1989. He was strict and unforgiving, but I am so grateful to him, as he set me up well, especially for right arm technique - my gosh, he was relentless in his demand that this be immaculate.

During my time with Brian I played in his two chamber orchestras and toured Europe a couple of times, when I was 12 and 14. Unforgettable! Amazing venues, concerts with Ozim and others. I remember we had a wonderful class with Peter Schidlof from the Amadeus Quartet, a tutorial on a Mozart divertimento. Talk about clueless: I just thought: 'this guy is super elegant and knows what he wants'. He even came to our concert in Cologne. What a dude, surely, he had better things to do!

After Brian left Australia, I was rudderless for a while. Then I happened upon Julian Quirit, a pupil of Dorothy Delay. He set my "violin brain" alight. He fired my imagination. He was such a phenomenal player: he could show you how to do things, how to get this or that sound. I watched him like a hawk. Julian really loosened me up. He made me a better player.

At the same time, I was really getting deeply into the violinists of the past - particularly Nathan Milstein. All these old greats were burrowing into my brain, and I wanted to make THAT sound at any cost. One could but try!

Tell me your most exciting musical experience as a player and as a listener.

As a listener, there are two. Hearing Martha Argerich play the Ravel G Major Concerto in Berlin, is etched in my mind forever. I knew at the time, especially in the last few minutes, that I would never hear piano playing like that again.

The other occasion was a quasi-religious experience. It was in 2013 in Sydney. The Concertgebouw Orchestra was on tour with Jansons. It was the most intense concert - especially "Ein Heldenleben". That was straight from the Almighty. One of the encores was from Grieg's Peer Gynt, ' Solveig's Song' . This little gem was delivered with the same care as the main fare. Oh, the mood they captured, the pain. I was in tears after that.

As a player there are a few. Eleanor Lea and Hartmut Lindemann playing Mozart's Sinfonia Concertante with Corpus Medicorum was wonderful. Libby Wallfisch, Ben Martin and Niall Brown playing the Beethoven triple with ADO in Sydney. What a performance, especially Niall, particularly in the high registers - unbeatable. Then there was an amazing Brahms First Symphony in Japan, with Corpus Medicorum. God only knows why, but the conductor (Keith Crellin) hadn't really rehearsed this piece. The first run through was the concert. I remember the last minute: it was white hot. I had no idea what sound I was making but I knew that the energy was bang on. I could feel myself being swallowed up in that sound.

What does music mean to you?

In a word, everything. Music is life, sun, oxygen. Music tells you about the gamut of human experience. It's the cosmos.

You are one of the few people in the orchestra who genuinely could have become a professional musician. So, why did you choose medicine and not music when clearly you have such a deep passion for it?

That has two answers.

For one, my emigre parents warned me off it. All the usual things, that you can't earn a living, have a stable life and so on. Then there is missing the boat, the timing has to be right. To do well at anything, I think you have to form that skill at a particular time of your life.

What's more, I am not sure that I have the temperament to live the life of a musician. It's a strange life. I can only say this with hindsight, but I'm grateful that I'm not a professional musician. Had I embarked on that route, I'm pretty sure that, at some stage, I would've said, 'No, it's not for me'.

I think part of the reason would've been to not love music anymore in order to do it professionally.

Say you're an orchestral musician, there's an element of Tonight is Bruckner 5. I have to play all the notes in the right order, perfectly, for 80 minutes, that's my job. And the guy up there flapping his hands, 'Puts the music in'. I don't actually think that way, but I'm sure that it can eventually be ground into you.

I have a very good friend, Naoko. She plays associate principal viola in the Berlin Philharmonic; she is at the top of her game. I saw her after one of their concerts, to go for a drink. I said, 'That was a phenomenal concert.'

'Was it? I was too busy playing.'

I remember another chat we had. She was rostered off for a week. Harnoncourt was conducting Schubert, but she went to the concert. In the most measured tone, she told me that this was when she realised that the Berlin Philharmonic were "quite good". Good god!

That doesn't entirely answer your question but gives a certain insight, I think.

Can you remember things going wrong in a performance

Tonnes! One comes to mind. We were on tour with Finlayson's chamber orchestra 'The Australian String Ensemble' in Slovenia - and we were running late. There was a visa irregularity at the border with Austria, we were turned back. Eventually we arrived on the outskirts of Ljubljiana - in the boondocks. We were going to play a program with Igor Ozim. One member of the orchestra came on with no shoes because they were left in Austria. The performance started higgledy-piggledy. I remember sitting there playing continuo and thinking, "Crap! I'm playing in the wrong key!".

What are your Desert Island choices?

Oh Miki! There are 5,000 of them! In terms of violin - Milstein, Milstein, and more Milstein. His recording of the Mendelssohn with Steinberg, so carefree; an incredible stereo version of the Glazunov with Frühbeck de Burgos, the slow movement, it melts; probably the best Lalo Symphonie Espagnole ever recorded, and the Goldmark concerto. He makes the music sound better than it probably is. The best. In terms of chamber music: Suk, Katchen and Starker playing the Brahms trios. I couldn't be without all the Bach Cantatas as recorded by Suzuki. In terms of piano: Géza Anda playing the Opus 25 Etudes by Chopin - it is sooooooo personal, like he is playing just for you. Good helpings of Miles Davis, Oscar Peterson, Sarah Vaughan, and

Ella Fitzgerald. I could go on and on - I'd need an ocean liner to haul all the stuff and a bloody big island.

How much are you practising at the moment?

I play very intermittently, according to "food and water." The New Zealand Doctors Orchestra (NZDO) is the one thing that keeps me going. Gigs are few and far between, so I dust off the beast and I have a play as I need.

How did you find out about ADO?

I remember seeing something on ABC news. It was a concert by Dvorak 8. Then I forgot about it. In 1998 I called you; you told me it was too late for me to register - but after some serious pleading, I got in!

And of course, we got you over to lead our premier concert in London with the European Doctors Orchestra in 2004 with Libby Wallfisch playing the Beethoven violin concerto.

That was a great gig, right up there as one my most memorable performing gigs. A blast!

ADO was so important in getting me playing again. Just before that gig in 1998, I had stopped studying with Julian and then, I stopped playing altogether. I was deep in "medicine, medicine, medicine, work, work, work". It happens but it's awful. In many ways, ADO and the Mt Buller Chamber Music Summer School saved me.

Dr. Anita Green

B Med Sci, MBBS, Dip RACOG, FRACGP

General Practitioner, French Horn

'Sometimes failures, but at least no-one dies!'

What are your earliest musical recollections?

Sitting at the piano at home having a lesson with my sister, who was teaching me how to play some simple tunes. She was 10 years older than me.

Do you remember the time when music first spoke to you?

That was at Taroona High School when I started learning the French Horn and joined the Hobart Orchestra. We performed a movement from Beethoven 7th Symphony. This was the first time I had played classical music and I caught the bug. I started off on trumpet at school and then during one of the lessons the music teacher asked me if I would like to change to French Horn. Might as well, it would be something a bit different" I thought. Taroona High School had and still has a big music program. We had a brass band and an orchestra during my time at the school as well as a variety of other instruments.

I started having lessons at school with Gwynn Williams who was a string player. He played the violin. I then joined the Tasmanian Youth Orchestra but one of the conditions was that I had to have a private teacher. I then started having lessons with Frits Harmsen who was the Principal Horn in the Tasmanian Symphony Orchestra.

My association with orchestral horn playing and the joy I experienced from it developed during my high school years as a member of the youth orchestra.

I did music for the HSC, but it wasn't on an instrument, I did music theory as a major.

What have been your most exciting musical experiences as a player, and as a listener?

We had a combined rehearsal with TSO when I was in grade 11. We played Mussorgsky's 'Pictures at an Exhibition'. We didn't have a tuba player to play the solo, so I was given the solo tuba part and at the end I received a big applause from the TSO players. So that was a pretty exciting experience for a young musician. When I lived in Darwin, we had some fantastic events with lots of outdoor performances with Darwin Symphony Orchestra. This included places such as the Daly River riverbed, Katherine Gorge where the orchestra and audience travelled up the gorge in army barges, Glen Helen Gorge where the fireworks set fire to the scrub, Nhulunbuy with Peter Sculthorpe on tour with us and Nourlangie Rock in Kakadu with guitarist John Williams as soloist in an all- Sculthorpe program. These concerts were conceived by Professor Martin Jarvis, the conductor at that time.

Mahler Symphony Number One was one of my favourite performances. My daughter Lana was only 12 weeks old and fortunately my husband Andrew was very supportive.

The Australian Doctors Orchestra has had some really memorable performances. The Saint-Saëns Organ Symphony that we performed in the Sydney Town Hall springs to mind. Holst "The Planets" and Rachmaninoff 1st Piano Concerto at the Gold Coast concert was another. I remember the Millennial Concert in Hobart playing Mozart's Sinfonia Concertante for wind instruments followed by Tchaikovsky's 1812 Overture with the brass band from Anglesea Barracks joining us. More recently Shostakovich 5th Symphony in Darwin was a special concert as we had moved to Hobart by then and it was a great opportunity to return to Darwin and perform with friends I hadn't seen for a few years. I remember the first ADO concert in Melbourne in Melba Hall, and I remember the conductor Chris Martin telling the horn section half an hour before the end of the final rehearsal that we had been behind the beat all weekend. I thought, "I wish you'd told us that yesterday." Happily, it all came together in the concert.

Our family used the ADO concerts as our annual holiday destination. We would pack the children up and fly off to wherever the performance was. Andrew would babysit while I rehearsed. Both of my children have gone on to be involved in orchestral and choral music and I think that these early experiences played a large part in their love of music.

As a listener my tastes have changed over the years. My earlier preference was for larger orchestral works with plenty of brass. I loved a good Mahler symphony, Tchaikovsky 4 and 5 and Dvorak 7,8 and 9. Hearing Barry Tuckwell and Herman Bauman perform as soloists were probably the most exciting performances I attended in my early days as a young horn player. I've had a lot to do with the Gondwana Choirs over the last 10 years since my daughter Lana and then my son Nicholas joined them. It's a national music program based in Sydney. Every January around 300 young singers aged 10-25yo come from all over Australia to the National Choral School. I have been volunteering at the camp as their doctor and also travelling with them on some trips overseas. As a result of this I've become more appreciative of and I have developed a love of choral music.

There have been some amazing concerts with them locally and overseas. The last one was in Berlin in 2019 where Gondwana Voices performed Brett Dean's 'Vexations and Devotions' with The Berlin Radio Orchestra at the Philharmonie. Here at home in Sydney they performed Mahler's Eighth Symphony with the Sydney Symphony Orchestra. As a parent I find now that the most exciting and emotionally moving concerts I attend are those in which my children are involved

Do you play any chamber music?

I am playing with the Derwent Symphony Orchestra in Hobart but chamber music? No, not really. I am busy with work and there are limited opportunities to play chamber music. We have a monthly get together with the horn players around Hobart and read through a variety of repertoire which makes for a fun evening. I had a friend come down from Darwin recently and he was pretty keen to do some chamber music, so we got a group together with Julian Bush and Murray Croswell. Murray and Julian and 3 others came to our Clunes Chamber Music weekend 4 years ago.

What does music mean to you?

Music has been a huge part of my life now for decades. I have played in horn sections with really wonderful people, and I have been able to travel the world. It has helped me fulfil many of the facets of being a human being. Playing the horn has always been a bit of a challenge for me because it doesn't come naturally. It has pushed me to achieve things that I didn't think I could do so it has provided a challenge for me. It's been great to have some successes, like pulling off a good solo in a concert. Sometimes there are resounding failures which can be a bit embarrassing but that's all right, at least no one dies! It's been a really important part of my life.

There was a time when I was doing as much music as medicine. Music speaks to me emotionally as well as providing a great social network. It has exposed me to some quirky personalities and helped me learn to negotiate difficult interpersonal relations. It is and has been an opportunity to be involved with my children in a creative and enjoyable environment. I have had great pride in hearing my children develop and perform. My daughter is embarking upon a career as a professional singer. She was clear from very early on that she wanted to sing. Music has taught both of my children that success in your pursuits requires dedication, focus, cooperation and hard work, all valuable life lessons.

Can you remember a time when things went wrong in a performance?

Yes, Tchaikovsky 'Waltz of the Flowers', I thought we were starting from the beginning but no, we were starting over the page just four bars before the horns introduce the theme. That was a bit of a scramble to get the page turned in time. I missed the first few notes but played most of it. The conductor was none too happy. Then there was the concert with the Tasmanian Conservatorium Orchestra in my early horn playing days. Two of us weren't playing in the first piece and we were told to wait downstairs at the back of the concert hall but they forgot to come and get us. There were some fairly important horn parts at the beginning of the second piece. We snuck on stage behind the percussion section and the conductor seemed pleased to see us.

What would be a Desert Island choices?

I would have to have my horn with me. I would take Elgar's 'Nimrod', Beethoven's 7th Symphony, the two Strauss horn concertos as well as the Mozart horn concertos so I could have another go at mastering them all.

For listening to I would like Mahler One, Dvorak Seven, Eight and Nine , Holst's 'The Planets" and a couple of my Gondwana and Voces 8 recordings.

Is there anything else you would like to talk about?

One of the really great things I've seen happen with my two children is that they have taken up music as well. It's been wonderful to see one play the violin and sing and the other pursue a career as a singer. It's been gratifying to watch them develop and for me to be involved with them and to see the baton being handed on. I am not a singer but their father sings. He is Latvian and music has been a part of his life. It will be a great day when the benefits of music are finally recognised and valued in this country.

Can you remember anyone significant in your musical life?

Frits Harmsen has been a key person in my musical development. He gave me a really good foundation. The wind players of the TSO who took us for tutorials in youth orchestra gave us invaluable guidance as young musicians. Alex Grieve who joined ADO for concerts in Melbourne was a mine of useful titbits of advice. Alex always had a lot to contribute and was an inspiration, he just loved his music and kept playing for years and was happy to help in any way.

Martin Jarvis as the conductor of Darwin Symphony Orchestra provided opportunities to perform in some extraordinary places. Keith Crellin who conducted the Tasmanian Youth Orchestra and TYO2 when I first joined. You Miki, when you founded ADO and gave us all an opportunity to play in an ensemble of such a good standard. It gave us that bit of extra inspiration to keep playing and make the effort to go along knowing that you're going to be involved in a good performance and have great musicians around you.

What make of instrument do you have?

I play an Alexander, made in Germany. They make really good horns and are very popular. We had a community concert with TSO recently and four of us had Alexander horns. The concert was a TSO initiative. They asked for expressions of interest from players within the community to go and rehearse then perform the last movement of Tchaikovsky's Fourth Symphony as well as a piece by Maria Grenfell.

How much do you practise?

It depends on what's coming up. I practised a lot for the TSO gig, and I have a big concert coming up that will require a lot of preparation. I can go for weeks without practising but recently I've been doing four or five hours a week. When I was in Darwin playing principal horn, I'd be doing four or five hours a week regularly as well as orchestral rehearsals.

How do you manage to practise with the big sound a horn makes?

In Darwin we lived on a five-acre block, and no one complained. Now we live in the same street that I grew up in and they're all used to it. The house is on half an acre. Actually, the sound doesn't carry all that much and I practise within reasonable hours.

What are they, what are reasonable hours?

In the morning after seven, but usually by nine, in the evenings I stop by 9 o'clock.

Dr. Bonnie Fraser

MBBS, FRACGP

General Practitioner, Percussion

'Music Transcends all Barriers'

What was your earliest music musical experience?

I remember sitting at the piano aged about five with Mum trying to teach me to play.

Was she a pianist?

Not professionally, but she went through most of the AMEB grades.

How proficient did you become on the piano and how did you become a percussionist?

I reached grade five on the piano and then when I got to high school, I was looking for an instrument to play again. My best friend in high school also played piano very well. They needed a couple of people in the school orchestra to play percussion, and having learnt the piano was an advantage, as they needed someone to play the xylophone and the xylophone's keys correspond to the piano keyboard. My friend went on to learn trumpet and I decided to have proper private lessons on percussion instruments at school.

Do you remember when music first spoke to you?

Towards the end of primary school, I started composing a bit and then later at high school I did music composition in year 12 rather than music performance as a subject. I think music really started speaking to me then as a means of expression and giving me the ability to craft something and put it together as a piece and submitting it for my SACE (South Australian Certificate of Education) was important to me.

What was your most exciting musical experience?

It was a special moment for me when I played my composition at the year 12 music night. It was a solo piano piece. I get very nervous when I have to perform, especially when playing in front of about five thousand people as I was that night! As I approached the stage, I suddenly realised that no one actually knew this piece and I'd be all right whatever happened.

I also wrote the music as a gift for my husband when I walked down the aisle at my wedding, which made the moment even more special.

How about as a listener?

I remember some really beautiful renditions of music, like, when one of the year 12's sang "Send in the Clowns" as a solo. The first time I heard Barber's "Adagio for Strings" it brought a tear to my eye as it was so beautiful.

The music at our school was wonderful; I thought of music as a sanity subject.

What does music mean to you?

I think it's a way of connecting with people; it's a form of the expression that you can't always put into words. It transcends all barriers and is a deep form of emotional expression.

When did you join ADO?

I was in first year medicine in Adelaide and ADO was held here in 1998. There were notices up in the Medical School foyer about joining an orchestra. I thought, 'What the heck, I'll give it a go'. Then I realised it wasn't just Medical students but mainly consultants from different specialties. It was amazing to see these big-scary-consultants have a totally different side to them. We hadn't even started attending the hospitals at that stage.

What happened career-wise after that? How do you fit your music in with your work-life? Do you belong to an orchestra?

I did a Navy scholarship through Medical School that put me through. I did my intern and residency at the Queen Elizabeth Hospital and then after my residency year, I went off to attend bootcamp and worked as a naval doctor for a few years.

Unfortunately, during the initial military training, I was injured, and I have ended up with chronic pain. I am now in general practice and not surprisingly have an interest in chronic pain and mental health. I've done the mental health level two training and do focused psychological strategies with patients, which I've found really useful for helping patients with chronic pain.

Frustratingly, the chronic pain has really limited my ability to play because I can't stand for too long. During Medical School, I was in the Burnside Symphony Orchestra until my intern year. I haven't been in a regular orchestra apart from the ADO since leaving the Navy.

I played keyboard in a rock band for a few years. This started from a cafe which was across the road from one of our practice locations. They had a piano and there were a couple of guys who'd bring their guitars and on one of my visits one of the guys said. "We're actually looking for a keyboard player for our band, would you give it a go? We rehearsed weekly, with some performances at local pubs; one of these performances was how I met my now-husband. After a while the band broke up. Then two years ago, a couple of people from the old band looked me up and till May this year I was playing with them and performing in local pubs again.

Did ADO bring you back to playing in a group?

Oh, definitely. It reignited my interest in classical music as well. It's difficult as a percussionist to have a chance to practise or to play regularly, and I've really enjoyed that.

Do you have percussion instruments?

Only small instruments as timpani are very expensive and take up a lot of room. I used to have a drum kit. When it comes time to practise, I get out of the practice pads, and pretend that they are the timpani. You don't hear or get much feedback, it's more to get the rhythm and the sticking right (i.e., which drum to hit with which hand).

I used to get picked out going through airport security on the way to ADO concerts, as I'd carry a small kit with me such as triangle, castanets, tambourine and a selection of mallets – 'So you're a professional triangle player, are you? (snigger)'.

What about when you play xylophone? I suppose that's not that hard because you're playing the piano, right?

Yes, that's right. When I have to learn the xylophone part, I'll get out my mallets and try it on the keyboard to work out the notes and patterns.

Can you remember when anything went wrong in a performance?

More than I'd like to admit! I was in the orchestra for a musical at high school, I was playing the glockenspiel. We didn't have a proper trap table, and so I was using a heavy music stand with the glockenspiel on it. The double bass player walked past with her double bass, and two seconds later, the whole of it flipped over. To this day, one of my friends still greets me with "crash! tinkle, tinkle, tinkle".

You were talking about percussionists having to count lots of bars before; I will never ever forget the look on Chris Martin's face in the rehearsal before a performance when I had quite a lot of bars to count in the symphony and got lost. Although they had cues, unfortunately, the person who put them in didn't realise that that particular phrase was repeated and so it wasn't a very clear cue. I thought I had worked it out and came in but not very confidently, Chris looked over and encouraged me to play louder and louder with bigger and bigger circular hand movements, then looked down at his score with his hand movements still going and realised I had come in eight bars early! It was never discussed after that, but fortunately it was fine in the performance.

Would you like to say anything about your experiences playing with ADO?

It's been a wonderful, warm experience, I remember going out for lunch with a couple of the doctors and seeing a totally different side to them. Some of the consultants are intimidating in the hospital at work, but then you see them at ADO and they are totally different. The atmosphere is always warm and welcoming and it's one of the things I've always really loved about it; I'm grateful for the opportunity to play as well.

The charity work is another plus and makes the whole idea less self-serving. I remember helping to organise the Sydney one in about 2000, while I was still in the Navy. That was a real eye opener to how much preparation goes into getting the ADO organised.

I am now ADO's webmaster and enjoy that involvement.

Are computers and programming an interest of yours?

Yes, very much so, I enjoy programming, creating websites and working on phone apps.

It's a bit like composing, in that with composing you can feed all the instruments into the computer program and then mix the instruments any way you like; the programming lets you end up with software that functions the way you want it to.

What are be your desert island discs choices?

That's a tough one! Probably Chopin, Barber's "Adagio for Strings", Debussy, a lot of the romantic era, or music with a lot of expression in it, as well as some jazz and blues. Of course, things you can sing / dance along to as well would be in there too!

There are great timpani parts in Dvorak's 5th Symphony and Stravinsky's "Firebird Suite" which I love listening to.

Did you have any significant figures in your life who influenced you regarding your love of music?

Definitely my mother, listening to her play at an early age was very inspiring, also, my friend Annie at school, as she had more exposure to different types of music than I had. She was a brilliant musician, it was amazing to watch her play and I joined the orchestra because of her.

The Power of Music and Musical Raspberries

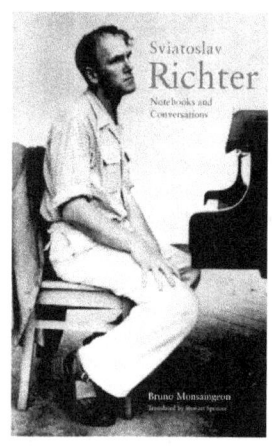

When the great Russian pianist Sviatoslav Richter was asked to play at Stalin's funeral he was delighted to accept. The Germans didn't like Richter because he was Russian, the Russians didn't like him because his name was German. What could not be denied is the fact that he was Russia's finest pianist.

The choice of music was his and it gave him the opportunity for revenge. It was a very brave choice because of all the famous Russian composers he could have chosen from he chose the greatest German Protestant composer of all time, J. S. Bach.

There were more than a few raised eyebrows. Wonderful!

The next story concerns the world's greatest Russian cellist Mstislav Rostropovich. He had a terrible time under the communists but his wife in 1974 saved him from becoming an alcoholic by moving to the USA.

When the cold war subsided, he was asked to return to the USSR with his American orchestra, which he was conducting. The concert was a great success, and an encore was demanded by the excited Moscow audience. The encore they chose to play was 'Stars and Stripes Forever'. How is that for another musical raspberry of mega proportions?

Rostropovich Is Home at Last with Just a Touch of America
By Craig R. Whitney, Special To the New York Times
Feb. 14, 1990

But it was John Philip Sousa's 'Stars and Stripes Forever," piquant piccolos and all, that had the whole great hall of the Moscow Conservatory clapping rhythmically to the National Symphony Orchestra's rousing rendition. This was the lighthearted end to a serious program that spoke in profound and instantly intelligible terms to the Russian audience - Samuel Barber's Adagio for Strings, Tchaikovsky's ''Pathetique'' Symphony and the Symphony No. 5 of Mr. Rostropovich's friend Dmitri Shostakovich, a cry from the heart at the height of Stalin's terror in 1937.

The attitudes and enthusiasm for classical music are stronger in Europe than elsewhere. This was beautifully demonstrated when Vladimir Horowitz, legendary pianist, returned to Moscow aged 82, having left at the age of 17. Not only were there queues in the street to get tickets for his recital, he was literally mobbed in the street!

Vladimir Horowitz

Dr Tony Prochazka

MBBS FFACCS(Med) FCPCA

Cosmetic Doctor, Cello

'Rostropovich himself said to me 'Intonation good, phrasing good, technique not bad - but your playing a little bit boring... but you're from Australia yes?'

What's your earliest musical recollection?

My earliest musical recollection is singing the chorus of 'She Loves You" by the Beatles in the prep school playground aged four, but the only words I knew were [*sings*] "Yeah yeah yeah"...

I was surrounded by music because my father played the piano and my mother the cello. My older brother played the violin but swapped to guitar about the time that Bob Dylan was starting to become famous. I think he figured it would help him to pick up girls. He may well have been right.

I started with piano lessons aged seven. You were told to do it so you just did it, just like going to school. I never really particularly enjoyed it, but I didn't mind the challenge and I got as far as learning the first couple of movements of a Beethoven sonatina. My mother said that when I played the piano, I was really banging on it. I was probably emulating the style of my teacher who had a percussive style.

So, after two years of thumping on the piano, my parents decided to swap me to the cello. My first teacher was John Kennedy, Nigel's father. My lessons with Kennedy were very different. It was very well known that he had an alcohol problem, so my parents always arranged for me to have the first lesson of the day when he was still in reasonable shape. I didn't know that at the time. I remember him being a very affable guy. I had a three-quarter cello, and I would play things from the Piatti books for cello that a lot of kids learned from. My mother told me later that after about my third lesson Kennedy said, 'You know, your son has a lot of talent, you should keep him going with this'.

After about six months I decided that I didn't like it. I thought that the cello had a funny smell and, and the rosin also, it was sticky. The cello was this big smelly thing, it was cold, and my fingers were cold, and the strings hurt the tips of my fingers and I didn't want to practise. I probably threw a tantrum and my mother's response was, 'Well, okay, so you want to give up, you don't want to play anymore, OK'. And I said, no, no, no, I didn't mean that - so obviously I did want to play. That was the turning point, and I realised that actually I like this. I started doing AMEB exams.

When I was ten our parents took the whole family to Europe. They deposited my sister and me in a Swiss international boarding school in Montreux for three months. At the time, of course I had no idea how privileged we were. They arranged for me to have lessons with a local teacher and hired a cello for me. I would sit up in one of the empty rooms on the top floor of this old school building after dinner to practise. There was no one around, but then people started coming into the room and asking, 'What are you doing'? 'I am playing the cello.' And I realised then that people were actually interested and liked hearing it, they liked hearing me play.

There was a school concert - I was about eleven. I played one movement of a Bach suite; I think it was the gigue from the first suite. I thought of it as 'Oh well, this is something you just have to do, get up there and play.' So, I got up and played and then I got this massive cheer from the audience which was a complete surprise to me.

At some point I changed teachers, as Kennedy was too far gone. I went with a guy named Arthur Bate who had been the principal cellist in the MSO for many years. He was retired by this point and just taught.

He suggested that I join the Melbourne Youth Orchestra. They were looking for another cellist, as someone had pulled out and they were just about to go on a European tour, which was to be their very first big overseas tour. I was not eligible because I was only twelve and the minimum age was thirteen, but management turned a blind eye. I was in the back desk, and I remember turning up to the first rehearsal. I'd been playing in the school orchestra, which was a pretty shambolic affair.

I turned up for the first rehearsal. I'd been given the music, it was Borodin's Second Symphony, I'd been practising it at home learning the notes. "Da - da - da - da - da - da - da…..DA". Okay, I think I can play this. The conductor raises his Baton…*DADADADADADADA-DA!!!* four times the speed that I thought it was played at. I hadn't played any notes at all, these things just came out of nowhere. I thought Oh S--T, I had better get my act together, I have to play at this speed!!!

That was an absolute eye-opener and my next major turning point because it was just so incredible. The experience of being in this orchestra with people who could actually play and being right in the middle of this overwhelming sound that I was helping create. I just loved it from then on, and then we went on the tour. We went to Italy, Salzburg, Vienna and London, and the tour ended in Edinburgh where we saw Leonard Bernstein conducting the London Symphony Orchestra playing Mahler's Second Symphony. These were the experiences I had at the age of twelve which made me realise how much I loved music. And so I just went from there, basically.

There was another MYO Europe tour when I was sixteen, and then I got into the Australian Youth Orchestra, and we did a tour of China in 1979. Laurien Kennedy (John's daughter) was leading the section and I was fifth cellist. The tour was amazing culturally because China hadn't opened up to tourism yet. It was pristine - 18 months after the Gang of Four had been deposed.

When was the watershed when you had to decide between music and Medicine?

I don't think there was ever a decision really. When I was 15, I was learning from Peers Coetmore who had been a cello soloist in England and then emigrated to Australia. She took my mother aside and said, 'Tony could be a professional cellist, he could even be a soloist but he's going to have to practise much harder". My mother then asked me what I thought. I said I didn't want to be playing the cello for three to four hours a day, it's too much. So that was that. But I didn't stop playing.

Then I got into Med School. I did the AYO China tour while I was in second year Med.

I was also playing the guitar in rock bands and decided that there were more women to be had playing the guitar than playing the cello, which is probably not true, but that's what I thought at the time. So, I abandoned the cello and went hell for leather at the electric guitar. That lasted right through Med School and into my intern year and a bit beyond. Brilliant fun, and yes, there were girls.

At some point I decided that I didn't want to be in hospitals anymore. In fact, I wasn't even sure I wanted to be a doctor at all. I was accepted into the Jazz course at the VCA as a guitarist. I learned jazz guitar for a year and then I picked up the cello again. The trouble with the guitar is that it's got a couple too many strings. Not only that, but the strings are also tuned the wrong way and I thought the guitar is not natural for me, the cello is my instrument. It was always my instrument. Why did I ever stop playing it?

Who were you playing with after finishing Medical School?

Through the jazz course I ended up doing a lot of jazz gigs, mostly playing guitar and occasionally cello. I had a residency for a while in a pub in South Melbourne, initially with Tony Gould, who was very well-known as jazz pianist and lecturer at the VCA.

Then what happened was: this guy was visiting the VCA. A visiting violin professor from Austria, based in Germany, Helmut Pfister came to take master classes at the VCA, and I played cello at one of them. He said 'Would you be interested in coming to Köln? I am very good friends with Boris Pergamenshikov, I think you should audition for him.' I gave Helmut an audition tape to pass to Boris. I got a very nice letter back from Boris saying that unfortunately he couldn't take me because I was one year over the Hochschule's age limit - but I could have lessons with his assistant.

The next year I moved to Germany and worked there for a year with Boris's assistant Hans-Christian Schweiker, a very good teacher and fine cellist who later became a professor in his own right.

How did you support yourself during this time?

My mother had passed away and I came into a small inheritance, and I lived off that. I lasted in Germany for a year. I really didn't like living there. Germany didn't suit me for a whole lot of reasons, one important one being that I couldn't pick up girls. (This interview is making me sound like some kind of crazed Lothario, but in reality, I'm nothing of the sort.)

I arranged to audition for Raphael Wallfisch at the Guildhall School in London, and he accepted me. I ended up being offered a half scholarship. Once I moved to England, I could support myself by working as a sessional hospital doctor, because in those days Australian Medical graduates could automatically register with the GMC.

I was there for one year attending the Advanced Solo Studies course, which is a diploma level course at the Guildhall School, studying with Raphael. It was during that year that I competed in the fourth international Rostropovich Cello Competition, which was held in Paris.

That was the most terrifying thing I've ever done in my life. The panel of 10 judges included many famous cellists - Rostropovich himself, Frans Helmerson, Arto Noras (a Finnish cellist) as well as Raphael. Predictably, I didn't get past the first round. There were about 45 contestants, including quite a few who went on to big careers.

So, you can actually say that you have played for Rostropovich. That's pretty good.

Because it was his competition, he could dictate how everything should be run. At most international competitions, you never find out why you passed or failed. You couldn't have any direct contact with the judges, but he said, no, it shouldn't be like that, so all the contestants were allowed to approach the judges after the announcements had been made about who got through to the next round and talk to them. The judges had all made notes and would be able to give you their immediate feedback.

Rostropovich himself said to me 'You know, intonation good, phrasing good, technique not bad - but your playing a little bit boring… but you're from Australia yes?' I said 'Yes'. "I love your country; I love your country!'

Funnily enough a lady approached me while I was milling around in the foyer and introduced herself as an Israeli music journalist and she said, 'Oh, I loved your Bach, I think you should have won the Bach prize'. So that really made me feel very good. Even though I didn't win any prizes and I didn't get through to the second round, at least someone came up to me afterwards and said they liked my playing.

I remember Arto Noras, the Finn, God he was an arsehole. I had to play two pieces. Three movements of a Bach Suite, and the Lutosławski "Sacher Variation". Referring to that piece he said, 'The way you played this piece is very bad, the interpretation completely wrong, you know, the first two notes should be very grand, and you just threw them away, it's just wrong.' He very definitely didn't like my playing. But that was okay. I just kind of nodded, smiled and said, 'Well, thank you.' I wasn't going to challenge this guy.

Can you remember when music first spoke to you?

Yes, from my very first memories, because my brother was playing his pop records and my father was playing his classical records, so music was washing through me all the time. I don't ever remember a time when music wasn't interesting to me.

Tell me your most exciting musical experience as a player and as a listener.

There isn't a single one. I would say playing the Haydn D major concerto as soloist with Corpus Medicorum was a pretty amazing privilege; playing Mahler's Resurrection Symphony on the 10th anniversary of 9/11 in the Convocation Hall Maryland, just outside Washington, DC with the World Doctors Orchestra, (WDO) - that was overwhelming. There were other special concerts as well, again with WDO playing Beethoven's Ninth Symphony in Berlin. With the Australian Doctors Orchestra, there were many, many great concerts, but I can't think of a specific one.

As a listener: the Leonard Bernstein concert in Edinburgh conducting Mahler 2 with the LSO. They had come up from London where they had just recorded it, and that is considered by some to be the greatest recording of the Resurrection Symphony. Miles Davis playing in Melbourne in 1988. Other great jazz concerts included hearing the Dizzy Gillespie quartet when I was 15 as well as Oscar Peterson with Joe Pass, and Stéphane Grappelli who all came to Melbourne.

I also attended a Rostropovich recital in 1988 and that was amazing as well.

What does music mean to you?

It's the single most important thing in my life outside of family and work, I guess. I'd have to say that music is more important than work - it's a lot more important than work. I would just wither away and die without music.

Can you remember a time when things went wrong in a performance?

It's very difficult to think of a time when things *didn't* go wrong in a performance…There was a classic one with WDO on a tour of China. We had a special piece that had been written for us by a Chinese composer. It was about a five-minute piece - a fanfare of sorts. The first performance was in Beijing, and it went beautifully. However, a day later we played the same concert program in Shanghai - where I was living at the time. Somehow the piece fell apart. The conductor of that orchestra is an incredibly musical guy, but he is not a professional conductor. He was always well-prepared, and he had a very clear beat, but if something goes badly wrong a pro conductor can reign it in.

I think there was a brass entry with a change of tempo; the brass launched into a tempo that was completely wrong and everyone else was playing it the way they played it the night before. He couldn't put it back together, so for the rest of this piece, there were two different tempi. We were all trying to find which tempo was going to dominate, jumping from one to the other - it got more and more fragmented until nobody knew where they were at all.

It kind of lumbered on for a few more minutes until suddenly everyone stopped playing. It was really bad. I mean, it was disgracefully bad, it couldn't have been worse. That was agonising, I didn't know whether to laugh or cry. I think I did both.

What are your desert island choices?

Obviously, the Schubert String Quintet, all of the late Beethoven quartets, Mahler's Resurrection Symphony, Beethoven's Choral Symphony. Then, there'd be a lot of jazz recordings and rock as well, but, you know, possibly none that a lot of people would have heard of. I don't listen to much rock and roll anymore. With jazz, it's just more like whatever comes to hand really because with recorded jazz it's nothing like actually being at a live concert seeing and hearing people compose on the fly, which is what you're doing when you're improvising in a jazz performance, there is a spontaneity in jazz that simply can't be captured on a record so I wouldn't put any jazz in.

How much do you practise?

That goes in fits and bursts, so I might go for months without touching the instrument but just lately I've been playing, because of lockdown, up to three hours a day. It also depends on whether I've got something to prepare for. During lockdown I decided to learn all the pieces that I should've learned many years ago. So last year during the first Australia-wide lockdown I learnt the cello parts of the Brahms Double Concerto and solo cello part to Richard Strauss' Don Quixote, and this year I have worked through the Elgar Cello Concerto, and I am now struggling through Henri Dutilleux's "Tout Un Monde Lointaine...", which is without question, the most difficult piece of music I've ever tried to learn, there's no question about that at all.

I forgot another peak musical experience was performing all of Bach's six Cello Suites in Shanghai, in one concert. The day before I was going to play, I emailed my old teacher Raphael  Wallfisch to say that I was doing all six Cello Suites in Shanghai. He sent an email back saying, that's funny, I'm playing all of Bach's Suites in London tomorrow.

I've seen both Pieter Wispelwey and YoYo Ma perform them in one sitting, it's a bit over two and a half hours of playing, and they played it from memory. I didn't. That could be a good project. I'm always up for a challenge…

Miklós (Miki) Pohl OAM

MBBS, FRCS, FRACS

Plastic Surgeon, Violin, Viola
Founder of ADO

'ADO allows musical-medicos to return to playing, we're big into salvage'

My earliest musical recollections were all in Budapest when I was four, with Mum in a tram. Apparently, I was singing a Hungarian folk song. A professor from the Liszt Academy overheard me and told my mother that I had a good ear and that I should learn an instrument.

Father and Uncle Gyula would meet on weekends and listen to records from Uncle's vast collection. Hungarian radio was continually broadcasting highlights from operettas by Kálmán, Erkel and Lehár. I know all the best tunes from 'The Merry Widow' and the 'Csárdás Királynö' as well as others.

When I was five or six, my godfather Vékes János took me to the ballet at the Budapest Opera House where we saw Tchaikovsky's Nutcracker and Swan Lake. I was mesmerised: the music, the dancing, the sets, the beautiful swans, the giant nutcracker soldiers, and the rats, are etched into my memory.

My mother decided I should play the violin.

At six I began lessons with Gyuribácsi (Uncle George). Gyuribácsi was a violinist in the Budapest Opera. He had old-fashioned ideas about teaching the violin. On arrival I would greet him at the door, he'd bend down for a kiss……very Hungarian. Kisses exchanged; the lesson began. If I didn't flex my left wrist enough, he would wedge a sharpened pencil between my wrist and the neck of the violin. This wasn't too uncomfortable as long as I kept my wrist flexed. His other "technique" was bloody painful. If I made a mistake, he would pull my right sideburn while I was still playing. This was supposed to encourage correct bowing, rhythm and intonation. A tear would roll down my right cheek, but I continued to play. I was never rewarded for playing well. Despite all this, I recall Gyuribácsi with fondness, most Hungarians are like that, they like to suffer.

Music first spoke to me when I was about five, I remember I had 2 favourite pieces that Uncle would play for me whenever I asked him to. They were Von Suppé's Light Cavalry Overture and a virtuoso violin piece called 'The Hot Canary' which had a great tune, as well as that, and no doubt played by a Gypsy Primás (leader), there were violinistic pyrotechnics where the canary's whistling and beak chirping sounds were emulated near the bridge of the instrument.

We arrived in Australia July 1957. Our first ten weeks were spent in Maitland NSW with my father's oldest brother, Uncle Frank, who was our guarantor. Mum and Dad quickly gained employment as leather goods tradesmen in Newcastle, their weekly wages were £7. With her first pay Mother bought me a half size violin and found me a teacher at the local Convent. My parents had always valued education and gave it the highest priority. W had nothing at the time except the clothes we were wearing.

At thirteen I auditioned as an external student to enter the Sydney Conservatorium of Music. Although I had no clue about auditions or the process' I gained entry. My big brother chose Errol Collins to be my teacher. He based his choice on the teacher with the most degrees after his name.

Erroll was not only my teacher he also became my mentor, confidant and friend. After an hour with him I always felt better about myself, my playing and the universe.

Music Is Medicine

We worked our way through the AMEB syllabus and I did well in my final exam. I was fifteen; my focus shifted to gaining entry into Medicine. The violin was laid aside for two years till I finished high school.

During orientation week in Med 1, I met Ben Freedman, the beginning of a lifelong friendship. Ben introduced me to the British Motor Corporation's National Youth Orchestra. We were in the first violin section.

Years later my training took me to Winnipeg, Canada. On arrival I went looking for fellow musicians and I met an orthopaedic surgeon named Mészáros. He invited me to join his string quartet and at the end of our conversation he paused and said....'You won't tell anyone will you.' I replied 'No, your secret is safe with me.' He was referring to his name which in Hungarian means 'butcher'...I have kept his secret safe till now.

Ben Freedman and me playing Bach Double Violin Concerto, Sydney 1980

On arrival in Hobart in 1982 I joined the Derwent Symphony Orchestra (DSO) which rehearsed under the direction of Martin Jarvis at Battery Point's historic St. George's Church. Martin, previously a professional violist with the Hallé Orchestra in Manchester, was a ball of energy and enthusiasm.

As it was coming up to JS Bach's 300th Birthday I suggested we celebrate with the 'Double Violin Concerto'. Malcolm MacLeod played first violin and I, second. The performance in the Hobart Town Hall went well. The Hobart Chamber Orchestra was formed later. With Phillip Taylor as artistic director for more than 10 years many fine concerts followed. Other conductors included Myer Fredman, Jean-Louis Forestier, Christopher Martin, Gary Wain, Joseph Ortuso and Peter Tanfield the current director.

'There are 51 weeks between Bullers'

In 1993 I finally managed to get to the Mt Buller Summer School for strings (MBSSS) with a quartet we had formed in Hobart. Without any shadow of a doubt the Buller week became the highlight of my year. It was at the 1993 Buller Summer School that the Australian Doctors Orchestra was born. I noticed a disproportionate number of participating doctor-musicians. The stars were aligned, and Christopher Martin and Rowan Thomas were also there. Chris was a professional violist and Rowan, an anaesthetist and exceptionally gifted violinist who had already been the cconcertmaster of three community orchestras in Melbourne. I asked Chris if he would be Australian Doctors Orchestra's Artistic Director and Rowan if he would lead it; both accepted enthusiastically.

I started recruiting immediately and rang every musical medico that I knew. Everyone knew of someone else who played an instrument. Before we knew it, we had 73 players. I can't describe the immense relief and joy I felt when I heard that first chord played at rehearsal. As soon as I heard it, I knew we would be all right.

The premiere concert was held in September 1993 to a full house in the Melba Hall at the University of Melbourne. The recipient charity was the Multiple Sclerosis Society. The orchestra is entirely self-funded, participants put in to cover all our costs enabling the

Jan Sedivka, Caitlin Williams, Karen McCrone, Beth Pennington, Beryl Sedivka, MJP / MBSS 1995

Founding members of ADO: Phillip Antippa, MJP, Rowan Thomas. Taken in St Petersburg, on tour with Corpus Medicorum

door takings to be passed on to the charity. This is a win-win as it brings an audience as well as helping generate funds for good causes, otherwise it would be too self-serving. Of course, families and friends of the players also boost the numbers.

Now in its 28th year, the orchestra has raised over $500,000 for various medical charities. We've been fortunate in having wonderful professional soloists play with us. We have since performed in every capital city in Australia as well as numerous country centres such as Newcastle, Bendigo, Ballarat, Port Macquarie, Mt Gambier and Healesville.

The camaraderie is one of the best things about ADO, as is providing the opportunity for musical medicos to return to playing. For many, it has become the highlight of their musical calendar. Some base their annual family holidays around it.

It was fun organising the first twelve ADO concerts. I then handed the reins to Cathy Fraser, a Sydney based Psychologist-GP-Flautist. She's done a marvelous job. Several others have been in charge since then. Our current president is Anna Glue (cello), doing a fine job in the face of continuing Covid lockdowns. Our database, with more than 1,000 members, continues to grow. We welcome dentists, medical students and all allied health professionals including physios, nurses, speech pathologists and music therapists.

In the pre-Covid years we gave two concerts annually with ADO. I also play with Phillip Antippa's Corpus Medicorum which gives three to four concerts annually. Once a year, I play with the European Doctors

Miklós (Miki) Pohl OAM

Orchestra in the UK, but that is also on hold. I recently joined the U3A Orchestra as well as the Whitehorse Orchestra. I love chamber music and hope that I will soon be able to play with my friends.

In 2015 we started ClunesMusic, a chamber music long-weekend held in beautiful Clunes, in country Victoria. It is modelled on the Buller Summer School. It's shorter, running for three days and three nights but still lots of fun. I can now claim I've played on ABC Radio - during an interview about ClunesMusic, in Ballarat.

Musical highlights as a player would have to include playing the Bach Double Violin Concerto with Malcolm McLeod in Hobart. Playing Mahler 2 with the European Doctors Orchestra in Belfast in 2016, as well as the Schostakovich 5 with Corpus Medicorum, and Chris Martin conducting Vaughan Williams 'Fantasia on a Theme by Thomas Tallis'.

When I play the G Minor or the C Major viola quintets the hairs stand up on the back of my neck, the only place I still have hair! Hartmut

Five Friends, Viola Quintet
(L to R) Rowan Thomas, Ben Davis, Barbara Oakes, MJP, Ian Goding

Katie McNamara and me on ABC Radio Ballarat at first ClunesMusic 2015

Lindemann stayed with us in Hobart when he was on tour with the Australian Chamber Orchestra (ACO). He invited three professionals from the TSO to play Mozart's C major viola quintet. I played second violin, a true highlight. Another highlight was Phillip Taylor conducting a performance of Fauré's Requiem in Hobart with Hobart Chamber Orchestra.

As a listener, Mahler 1 with the MSO conducted by Hiriuki Iwaki and Mariss Jansons conducting the Concertgebouw SO with in Melbourne's Hamer Hall a few years ago. My first Buller with the ASQ (Hennessy, Lea, Crellin, Laurs), who played Schubert's 'Death and the Maiden' as well as Schubert's Cello quintet with Christian Wojtowicz.......I can't stop!!!! Oh yes, at the BBC Proms, Gergiev conducting the Mariinsky SO performing Shostakovich's Fourth Symphony. Erik, only 14 then, and I both came out of the concert as though we'd been struck by lightning!

My desert island choices would include Bach, in any shape or form, especially his six Brandenburg Concertos and the solo violin and cello suites. Any Beethoven string quartet played by the Végh Quartet. As I love choral music, I would include De Lassus, Tallis, Schütz, Monteverdi, Byrd, and the great romantics Brahms, Mendelssohn, Tchaikovsky, Beethoven, Sibelius, Richard Strauss, and many more, I can't stop!

Miki and Tom Samek

Dr Anna Glue

MBBS, FRACGP, DRANZCOG, DA

General Practitioner, Cello
Past ADO President

'It is tragic in this country that all children do not have access to a musical education. It gives them another language with which to express themselves. It is also a great skill to have, as ADO shows that you don't have to make music your career. It's a great way of becoming involved in your local community, whether in a choir or a musical theatre or an orchestra.'

What was your earliest musical recollection?

My earliest musical recollection is playing the recorder at school and at home. I also remember my parents had friends over regularly and they would play recorder quartets and ensembles. So, I learnt the recorder at home, rather than at school. Interestingly, I cannot remember learning to read music. It's something I learnt as I was learning to read. I was about six or seven.

Was there much music in the house?

My parents had learnt the violin in their youth, neither continued to play after that. Mum played the piano a little bit but there was music on the radio and lots of records. We listened to ballet music and my sisters and I could dance to that. My grandparents were classical music enthusiasts and they were Friends of the MSO and often hosted visiting conductors or musicians at their home.

One of my earliest concert recollections is going with my grandfather to hear Dvorak's cello concerto in the Melbourne Town Hall. I was 11 or 12 and I was already learning the cello then.

At what age did you start learning the cello and why did you choose it?

I started in grade five when I was 10 or 11. I had already been learning the piano for a year. My parents insisted that my sisters and I had to study two years of piano so that we would be fully musically literate. After that we could play whatever we liked at school. The school was offering free string lessons for two terms and I chose violin, but they had too many violinists, so I was given a cello.

Who did you learn from in Melbourne?

I learnt from Anne Baxter at school, and I did HSC music performance in year 12. Later, as an adult I took lessons for 10 years from Miranda Brockman, an MSO cellist, as she lived only 20 minutes from us.

Did you have a gap in your playing?

I never had a really big gap. COVID has caused the longest gap I. As a medical student I played at university with the Monash University Orchestra which I was involved in starting from 1982.

After I finished uni I played with Collingwood Chamber Orchestra which later became Melbourne Symphonia. Rowan Thomas also played with them. Then I went to Taunton in the UK for a couple years on rotation from Box Hill Hospital doing a diploma in anaesthetics as part of my GP training.

I didn't have my cello, so borrowed one and joined a community orchestra for 12 months. When we came back from the UK, I had a small child and I rejoined Melbourne Symphonia for a while. Then we moved to Ballarat and since being here I've often played with the Ballarat Symphony Orchestra, as well as pit orchestras for local theatre companies. More recently I've played with the Geelong Symphony Orchestra because it's not far from here. We started a string quartet after the Geelong ADO concert where we all met. I also play in Corpus Medicorum and ADO of course.

Have you got special interests within general practice?

I do quite a lot of women's health and menopause and some doctors' health.

Do you get to play some chamber music?

Not at the moment because the other members live in Geelong and Hamilton and every time we try to meet there is another lockdown restriction. It's hard when you live in different towns across the state.

When does music speak to you?

That's a tricky question because it's just there all the time. I don't always have music playing, but I often have music going in my head. We were looking back on early videos we took of our oldest son as a child, as we were sending them back to my parents from the UK. There was background music playing in every video. We hadn't realised how much we had unwittingly exposed our children to music, which was the way I was raised as well.

An AHA! moment was listening to the Melbourne Symphony Orchestra playing Aaron Copeland's Third Symphony. There is a fanfare in it when the whole brass section stood up and played, it was amazing.

Were you tempted to play brass?

Actually, I learnt the French Horn for a couple of years when I was at school but no, I wasn't tempted to change to brass.

Does Mark, your husband, play?

No, but he's been very supportive of me and the children playing. He is great and comes as an audience member and supports us that way. I think it would be very hard to keep playing if your partner was not supportive. He will come to concerts and put up with those which are not as good as others. One of our kids said one of the nicest things to me, as I had a concert in Melbourne and I said, "Look, you don't need to come to this concert, you've got work to do". When they were small, I used to insist that they come. He said, "Well, I'd like to come, besides that's what we do in our family, we support each other when they're doing things that are important."Mark derives enjoyment going to concerts and he's got a much better understanding of music now, so I don't think it's just a one way thing.

What was your most exciting musical experience as a player and as a listener?

The Aaron Copeland was one as a listener. We used to go to the MSO family concerts in the eighties. They were held at seven o'clock on Friday nights, as Family Fun Concerts, designed for young people, children, school-aged kids. My first "grownup" concert was with my grandfather who took me to hear Dvorak's cello concerto at the Melbourne Town Hall, I was 11.

As a performer there have been some really good ones. Beethoven's Ninth Symphony is always very exciting. So many people were on stage. I've played that with the Ballarat Symphony and Geelong Symphony. The other memorable concert was 10 years ago in 'Made in Ballarat' with Ben Northey conducting. We had David Hobson and Jackie Dark singing. I really liked the Shostakovich we did in Darwin with ADO. I also liked the Sibelius we performed with Ben Northey with Corpus Medicorum, as well as Holst's "The Planets".

What does music mean to you?

It's almost like another language, a language of emotion, happy, sad, good and bad. Often, I think of things in musical terms. There's happy music and there's music that always makes me feel really emotional. There are associations such as the slow movement of Mozart's clarinet concerto which always reminds me of my grandfather because he loved it so much. Beethoven's Ninth also reminds me of him because he used to say that this was not something you could play quietly. It had to be played loudly. Nimrod from Elgar's Enigma Variations, which was played for all of my children when they were leaving school. They are things of great emotion, it's not just classical music, there are songs that remind you of where you were, what you were doing, and who you were with at the time. Words and images don't do it like music can. We know that people with dementia respond often to music and that people who have lost the power of speech can sometimes still sing. I think music is a very special part of being human.

Tell me a bit more about your grandfather.

My grandfather was a lawyer who had his own law firm, but he was very involved in classical music, as was my grandmother. They were great supporters of the Melbourne Symphony Orchestra. I remember Hiriuki Iwaki was invited to their house. They held receptions for visiting conductors and soloists. Iwaki was one of those invited for a soiree. They attended a lot of concerts and they also insisted that their four daughters had basic music training, which was what my parents insisted on for me and what I have insisted on for my children. I think the gift of music is one of the greatest gifts we can give our children.

Can you remember when things went wrong in a performance?

Oh yes, I have one where things went terribly wrong playing in an orchestra. It was part of the Organs of the Ballarat Goldfields Festival. I was playing in a chamber orchestra with a conductor who I knew well, our soloist was playing the 'Poulenc Organ Concerto' and got lost, skipped a couple of pages and then skipped back a couple of pages, which meant we had no idea where the soloist was. The conductor had no idea. He'd signal 4 with his fingers. Was that rehearsal figure four or the 4/4 section? Anyway, we met up at the end. I don't know if the audience noticed. It was one of the most terrifying experiences I've had musically. The good thing was that there were breaks when it was just the soloist playing so the audience probably didn't notice, but it was scary to be completely lost.

Does Ballarat have a lot of music?

There is vocal music and singing. There are two musical theatre companies as well as a symphony orchestra and several brass bands. I've done pit orchestras for lots of shows. They'll do maybe 10, 12 performances over a two week period, so it's a busy couple of weeks but it's fun and a very different type of playing.

What would be your Desert Island choices?

The Bach solo cello suites absolutely. Sibelius's Second Symphony and I would probably put some music in there by Queen and maybe some jazz by Vince Jones.

You're the first to mention non-classical choices, which is great.

I listen to a wide variety of music.

How much do you practise?

Not much at the moment but usually a couple of times a week, I tend to practise leading up to an event. If there's not much on, I don't. I've not practised a lot the last 18 months, but coming up to a concert, I'll probably practise four times a week. I don't like playing by myself, that's why I play an orchestral instrument. I am very much goal oriented leading up to a concert or a rehearsal, but playing by myself doesn't really appeal.

Is there anything else musical you would like to talk about?

It is tragic in this country that all children do not have access to a musical education. It gives them another language with which to express themselves. It is also a great skill to have, as ADO shows that you don't have to make music your career. It's a great way of becoming involved in your local community, whether in a choir or a musical theatre or an orchestra. It brings many people so much pleasure and it's one of those things where the sum of the parts is always greater than playing by yourself. Playing in an orchestra is always so much better than playing by yourself, getting a sense of teamwork without it being competitive, as opposed to sport. It's a participation, not a competition. That's a really good skill as it gives kids confidence to get up and play an instrument in an orchestra or play an instrument in front of your class. You can speak, in public and you can present your projects so much better. So, I think we should be providing much better music education for everybody.

As ADO's current president......

During the pandemic I'm finding it really hard to organise events while having to change plans all the time. I already have to change plans the whole time at work and in my personal life and with the pandemic it's just so hard. It will be interesting to see how the orchestra comes out of COVID because it will probably be a very different orchestra. How might we do things differently? Like using local soloists and conductors so that if there are last minute restrictions, we have got our soloist and our conductors there.

When was your first ADO?

My first ADO was in Sydney in 1995. We played Elgar's Enigma Variations and Elgar's Cello Concerto and back then we only had two days rehearsal.

I well remember that concert, we only just made it and quickly went to 3 day rehearsals after that.

We pulled some variations because we were so short of rehearsal time. I was 10 weeks pregnant, so I wasn't feeling brilliant, but it was still good. I enjoyed the concert and the playing experience. I quite like the intense rehearsal schedule. Geelong Symphony rehearse a bit like that as compared to Ballarat Symphony who rehearse weekly for eight weeks.

Dr Jean McMullin

MB, BS

General Practitioner
Violin, Viola, Trombone

*'Music gives me pleasure
and a kind of energy'*

Jean, what's your earliest musical recollection?

My mother playing the piano. She was a good pianist and came from a very musical family. Her three sisters all played and sang, something they inherited from their father who was a baritone. They used to sing in four-part harmony around the piano after dinner. I had 3 older brothers, the first of whom was not interested in music; he probably took after my father who was tone deaf. My second and third brothers learnt the piano, and at the age of 3 I would go to the piano and play their pieces by ear. I remember the very first piece I played by ear called "Drifting". On hearing that, my mother thought, 'Well, we'd better get some piano lessons happening here.'

I first started learning from a lady whose name I can't remember; I was about five and used to go to her after school. She lived in Springfield Road just near my primary school. She was very encouraging, and I enjoyed my time with her. After a couple of years with her it was decided I should move on to the teacher my brothers were learning from, Roy Shepherd, a well-known teacher in Melbourne and a specialist in French

music. The three of us would be driven to his house in South Yarra on Saturday mornings, and the order of our lessons was dependent on the timing of my brothers' school football or cricket games. The lessons took place in a dark lounge-room with a modest shaft of morning light shining through small lead-light windows.

We had to sit quietly on some period furniture while the others had their lesson. Sometimes Mum stayed as well, or sometimes she would wait in the car. Mr. Shepherd was terrifying, and he would hit the back of your hand if you didn't play things correctly. I'll never forget the first time he got me to do aural tests. He didn't tell me what was about to take place, he simply told me to get off the piano stool, stand next to the end of the keyboard and to turn around to face away from him and the piano. I had no idea what was going on and kept turning back to see what was about to occur. I think I was afraid he was going to hit me or something. He turned to my mother and said, 'Curious, isn't she'.

Of course, once he told me to sing the upper or lower note of a chord or phrase, I thought it was great fun and wanted to keep doing aural tests for ever. He was so fierce that if the lesson didn't go well, our family coined the phrase that such a lesson was deemed a "roasting"!

Another happy memory from my primary school days was that after lunch each day when I was in prep and grade one, we had a rest time at school during which we would all lie down on thin foam mattresses and our teacher, an accomplished pianist, would play to us as we rested. She was my classroom teacher for both those years and sometime later as an adult when I came across her again, she found a letter I had written to her at the end of grade 1, wishing she could always be my teacher!

I moved to PLC (Presbyterian Ladies' College) from grade three, and in grade five, group lessons were offered in different instruments. I was already playing the piano and I had the honour of playing in assembly a couple of times. I started learning the violin with a group of four kids. We had a lovely teacher called Aileen Stooke. She is 95 now and still going strong. After about two terms she rang my mother and told her I was showing promise and should have individual lessons and that she should consider buying me a violin.

We went along to Mr Dolphin in Hawthorn. He had a workshop at the back of his house which was a converted garage, and I can still remember the smell of the rosin and the wood. I was 10 and we bought a full-size violin that cost $150, which was a lot of money then and I treasured it. I remember I used to play pieces with my brothers. They would accompany me and sometimes I'd get cross with them and hit them with the bow if they didn't get it right. I remember Dad paying me a backhanded compliment one day by coming up to me while I was practicing after about 2 years on the violin and saying 'I can recognise that tune, you're progressing well!' Dad was a great fan of Gilbert and Sullivan and would love it if I played "Poor Wandering One" with one of my brothers on the piano.

One day when I was about 11, I sat on my bow and it broke, it snapped in the middle, and I was pretty upset. I was very worried about what Mum and Dad would say, so unbeknownst to them I pulled out the pink pages, got on the phone to Allans Music and Brash's, and got some quotes for different bows. I then approached Mum and Dad and said, 'I've got bad news to tell you. I've accidentally broken my bow but I've rung around and got a few prices and I think this is the best buy. I think they were so impressed that I actually showed the initiative to do that research that they instantly forgave me, and we went and bought a new bow.

How serious and responsible were you as a young girl?

When I started senior school, I had to change violin teachers which was really upsetting for both me and Aileen. I was the leader of the junior school orchestra, and I really enjoyed it. I then had to take lessons from Judith Anderson who was awful. Luckily, Aileen conducted the senior school orchestra, so I still got to see her. I ended up leading the senior school orchestra from Year 8, which was a great honour because I was so young.

The instrumental teachers changed a lot over the next five or six years, so I had four or five teachers during that time and it was very unsettling. Every time I had a new teacher, they would favour a different methodology. So, you'd buy all the Sevčic books one year and then for the next teacher you had to buy the Dofflein books. I didn't progress that well and my technique suffered. Sometimes, because I was good at sight reading, I used to just wing it in the lessons and play through pieces fairly well when I hadn't even practised. I threatened to give up the violin, but Mum and Dad were against that. I was in year 11, and after some discussions we found a teacher outside school.

At that point I also started playing in the JSO-Junior Symphony Orchestra - which used to rehearse on Saturday mornings at Stonnington Teachers' college in Malvern. We had a conductor called Lindsay Knight and used to go to camps together. I remember working on Lieutenant Kije and Sibelius's 2nd Symphony amongst other things there. The social scene there was healthy and lots of fun, and that kept my interest in music going. I also went to National Music Camp at the suggestion of my teacher which I absolutely loved- I think I went at the end of my last year at school and also at the end of my first year at university. As university studies became more challenging, I found I didn't have time for the violin and I stopped playing after a while. I wasn't really aware of the Conservatorium orchestra and looking back I feel I missed a great opportunity there, because Chris Martin was conducting it at the time, I believe.

When did you reconnect with it all?

When I was a first year resident, there was a stop work meeting and the resident doctors went on strike. We had to go to Royal Parade in Parkville to this big car park which I think was under the AMA building and I remember an old friend from JSO coming up to me, Bronwyn Francis. She said, 'Hey, do you want to play in a quartet?' 'Oh yeah, that sounds great'. So, we started playing in a quartet regularly with another doctor and an OT, which was great fun. At the time, my 3 aunts were singing in the Caulfield Choir, and quite often they joined with other choirs such as Camberwell Chorale to put on a concert, such as a requiem or an oratorio. I think that is how I came to play in an orchestra called Camberwell Camerata, conducted by Doug Heywood, which provided the orchestra for these works. Doug is about 80 now, he's the guy on Carols by Candlelight who conducts the Alleluia Chorus each year.

I absolutely love the sound of a good choir, and the resonance that is produced by the blend of voices. I joined this orchestra in my residency year and had not played the violin seriously for a long while. I'll never forget the time when we had our first combined rehearsal with the choir, we were playing Elijah by Mendelssohn- and on hearing this huge body of sound that erupted after the orchestral introduction I felt a visceral shudder and a wave of goosebumps, thinking this is so wonderful and realising how much I had missed music during that period of disengagement when studying.

When did music first speak to you?

It was definitely as a child; music was all around me. My mother would often go and sit at the piano and play Chopin and Liszt, and I would hear my brothers practising. I was taken to church every Sunday- Presbyterian Church and later Uniting Church, and often sat between my parents with my mother beefing out a strong alto line , while my dad sang off key! My auntie Bet was a very accomplished soprano and used to sing solos in the church choir. I used to love the harmony of the hymns and had my definite favourites. Still to this day I can sing many hymns word for word. My brother Keith also learnt the organ and was very good at it. Every Sunday after church, while my parents were having morning tea in the church hall Keith, and I would sit at the organ and try to play the foot pedals. We would play through our favourite hymns with all the stops pulled out and of course played parts of the famous Toccata and Fugue in D Minor by Bach.

I remember at school, I was 13 and we were doing drama, we had to move around the room to 'Winter in Vivaldi's 'Four Seasons'. I remember thinking this is absolutely beautiful but no one else seemed to be particularly moved by it. A very simple tune, but just so harmonious and so enchanting.

My 3 unmarried maternal aunts were always interested in my musical ventures, perhaps even more than my mother. They lived together and used to spend a lot of time doting on us and closely following our musical and/or sporting (in the case of my brothers) endeavours. They would come over to our house every Saturday morning, and I remember that when we started playing Sibelius' 2nd in JSO which I loved, I couldn't wait to play them the LP album I had bought of it on one of these mornings. Auntie Kath knew it well and we both marvelled at the wonderful majestic and climactic ending of the last movement.

My aunts (Bet and Kath) used to travel a lot and I remember them going to see the Passion Play in Bayreuth, and both of them attended Dartington music festival in the UK on a couple of occasions. In 1986 I met up with Auntie Kath at Dartington and we both sang in the choir together in the mornings, and I also played chamber music in the afternoons whilst there. There were wonderful concerts every evening as well.

I started learning the violin again from Spiros Rantos when I was 26 or 27. I really enjoyed those lessons. You'd walk into their house in Templestowe and it was really chilled. You'd sit down and have a coffee with Bracchie and Spiros, who was very laid back and chatty while he had a cigarette, then about half an hour later, you'd go into the lesson in the music room and he'd put on his teacher hat and his whole demeanor changed completely. He was strict and theoretical and pedantic, a great teacher. A the end of the lesson, you might go out and have another little cup of coffee or something. The whole process took at least two hours. I did a couple of AMEB exams then. They might've been in seventh and eighth grade at that point.

Around that time I played in Stonnington, or Malvern Symphony as it was known then. I used to love it when Chris Martin conducted. I do remember some very special concerts with him, in particular Elgar's Sea Pictures, and Vaughan Williams's Fifth Symphony. I developed a fondness for all of the works we studied with Chris conducting; I think, you know, just his demeanor and his comments and obvious love for the works were quite infectious. Those were very special times.

What was your most exciting musical experience as a player and then as a listener?

I think as a player, Mahler's Second Symphony that we performed with EDO (European Doctors Orchestra) in Belfast was amazing. As a listener, it was after doing my medical elective in 1982. I had been in Nepal for three months without any classical music and was to fly on to another elective in Edinburgh. My parents were also travelling, as was one of my brothers, so we decided to have a week together in Austria.

You know that in Europe often they perform the Messiah around Easter time rather than at Christmas. We were in Vienna, and we saw that there was going to be a performance of the Messiah while we were there. We all went, and it was so amazing. That period of time in Nepal for three months without music heightened my yearning and awareness and goosebumps followed! Something happens to you internally, it's hard to describe, you know?

Another nice story about the Messiah was one of the last concerts I went to with my mother. She had been getting more confused. She wasn't too bad, but she definitely had cognitive impairment. It was Christmas time, and I thought she would enjoy going to Hamer Hall and hearing the Messiah played by the MSO and MSO Chorus. I shepherded her in with her frame ahead of the rest of the audience, and she sat upright and alert throughout the concert. She would have been in her late eighties, and she knew every word. She sang along the whole way and she was so uplifted by it. She was like a different person. That was pretty special.

What does music mean to you?

Music gives me pleasure and a kind of energy, it's one of the reasons to live. It surprises me how much it moves me; you could be driving along and suddenly something comes on that's just so beautiful that you lose track of where you're driving to. I've had that driveway phenomenon when you arrive at your destination and you're running late, but you can't bear to get out of the car because it's impossible to leave before the music finishes.

Music also evokes memories, similar to smells, transporting you in time and place. One Saturday when we were on our way to have piano lessons, my two brothers and I noticed my cat had been knocked over by a car overnight unbeknownst to us and was lying in the gutter. I would have been 10 at the time, and I was devastated. We still had to go to our piano lessons even though I was in tears. My brother at the time was working on a piece by Bartók, "Three Hungarian Folk Songs from the Csik district". Now, whenever I hear or play that music, I am taken back to that moment in time, with that feeling of my cat having just died, the association persists.

Like time travel.

Yes, it might remind you of a particular concert you were in, who you sat next to, how exhilarating it was and so on.

Dr Jean McMullin

How did you become aware of ADO?

Through people playing with the Stonnington Symphony, or possibly word of mouth.

I've got that wonderful photo of you in 1994 with one of your babies lying on a blanket by your seat and a play station to keep it occupied. That certainly showed your love of music and your dedication to playing.

Can you remember when things went wrong in a performance?

I do remember in a Corpus concert when the soloist lost his or her place in the Brahms Second Piano Concerto. I was quite thrown by that. Imagine how the conductor felt. It was Keith Crellin, I can still remember the look on his face as he was conducting! The soloist started improvising a bit like Keith Jarrett, and we all felt for him, but just to think it could actually happen was quite alarming.

Oh, I do remember another one which was the ADO Gold Coast concert. We were playing Smetana's "Moldau" and Holst's "Planets". The conductor wasn't happy with a few of the sections in the orchestra and the rehearsals weren't as light-hearted as usual. I've noticed that as you get older, you need to be more prepared before a concert. When I was younger, and working longer hours, I used to go off to orchestra without having even looked at the music and I just sight read at the first rehearsal. I don't think I could wing it these days!

But you were such a good player you could get away with it. When did you take up Viola?

I think I was in my thirties or forties. I think I was drawn to it from the years listening to the viola sound at Mount Buller Chamber Music summer school. The viola gets so much more exposure in the chamber music setting than in the orchestra and you can really hear that beautiful sound.

What are your Desert Island choices?

I definitely would like something orchestral and something choral. I think Mendelssohn's Elijah would be one, and Cantique de Jean Racine by Fauré would be another, it's absolutely beautiful. I would take Strauss's Four Last Songs and some Mahler, probably the slow movement of hisFourth Symphony. We played that with Corpus Medicorum, Sara (Jean's daughter) was in Melbourne at the time and she came and played cello with us. She sat with Ruth Saffir and that was pretty special because, with her living in Sweden, we don't have that many opportunities to play in the same ensemble.

Which string quartet would you take?

I am still getting to know the late Beethovens, they are very special. They would bring intellectual stimulation, but I am more drawn to the middle and earlier Beethovens. I love the Mendelssohns, and I love the Mozarts. Some Haydn would provide some humour!

Jenny Johnson was thought of as the matriarch of chamber music in Melbourne. Do you think you might have taken on that mantle?

Partly, I learnt a lot about chamber music from my friend Linda in England, who has been to Mt Buller two or three times. She knew a lot of quartets, their opus numbers and so on and I picked up a lot from her. I like to think that I have encouraged and introduced other string players to the chamber music fold over the years.

What are your thoughts about Australian Doctors' Orchestra overall?

I love working on a piece, getting it up to performance standard and it's also a great chance to see parts of Australia as well and the social side is fun. That whole process of working together on something, especially if you didn't know the piece previously, then uniting and performing it is a really satisfying process. Just the coming together, the combination of everyone concentrating with a common purpose, as well as supporting a local cause is highly satisfying.

Do you have a preference for the Violin or the Viola?

Although I like different things about both, I probably like the sound of a good viola over a violin. I love sitting in the middle of the orchestra next to the cellos. On the other hand, there is something exhilarating about playing the violin. If you are in good form and you're playing it well it's absolutely fantastic.

The highs and lows are different playing Viola. In orchestral playing I like both instruments equally but playing the viola in quartets is really special.

It's great to have a good tune every now and again and sometimes violas miss out on that. Having said that, violas get their moments in the sun as well. I am a bit torn; I love them both. Over the last couple of years, I have started having lessons on the trombone, which has opened up a whole new world for me, introducing me to the skills of breath control, tonguing and embouchure. It's a challenge, but I'm prepared to give it my best shot, and the best thing about it is that it equates to MORE MUSIC!

Music As a Means of Social Change, 'El Sistema'

Playing in his room, a 6-year-old boy is arranging his orchestra. The little figures in front of him are carefully organised, first violins on the left, seconds on the right, the conductor's podium at the centre. Behind, violas, cellos and at the back on the right, the double basses, further back the woodwinds and, behind them, the brass and percussion.

When he is finished, he goes to the kitchen, 'Grandma, could you please not touch my orchestra, leave it how it is'.

Dudamel

The greatest son of Venezuela's public musical educational system 'El Sistema' is Gustavo Dudamel.

Internationally famous, currently he is the principal conductor of the Los Angeles Philharmonic Orchestra, as well as the principal guest conductor of the Budapest Festival Orchestra.

Music As a Means of Social Change, 'El Sistema'

Most people have never heard of the Venezuelan, José Antonio Abreu. An economist, composer, conductor, and for a while member of Venezuela's parliament. In 1975, while holding the 'Minister for Culture' portfolio, he secured government funding to establish El Sistema.

El Sistema gives the opportunity for impoverished children to learn an instrument and join an orchestra. Commencing in small villages with basic instruments, orchestras were formed throughout the country. Children were selected from areas where there was a high prevalence of violence, drugs and crime.

There are many documentaries about Dudamel, Abreu and El Sistema. My favourite is The Simón Bolívar Youth Orchestra en route to the Salzburg Music Festival culminating in an amazing performance. That appearance brought them overwhelming international fame and success. The SBO was founded by Abreu in 1978, comprising well over 100 players, all brimming with talent. The orchestra has a beautiful warm sound, and with Dudamel conducting, it took the world by storm.

Dudamel with José Abreu

The documentary also traces little children from poor backgrounds being nurtured right through to holding important positions in world famous orchestras such as the Berlin Philharmonic, Vienna Philharmonic and many others.

Music Is Medicine

Music has to be recognized as an...agent of social development in the highest sense, because it transmits the highest values - solidarity, harmony, mutual compassion. And it has the ability to unite an entire community and to express sublime feelings.
Jose Antonio Abreu

When Abreu died in 2018, I shed a tear and I placed his image on my computer. A silent genius who made the world a better place, using musical education to achieve his goals.

By 2015 there were 400 El Sistema music centres throughout Venezuela that had trained 700,000 young musicians in their children's and youth orchestras. Twenty-five countries have adopted El Sistema since then.

Dudamel visited UAE in 2014. My son Nick was living there at the time with his family. Walty, my oldest grandson, was six at the time. I had played him his favourite track over and over, it's from SBO's Salzburg concert, Baba Yaga (The Witch), by Mussorgsky. Walty knew it backwards having conducted it since the age of two. Nick took him and Sari (Walty's sister) to the concert. It was in the Emirates Palace coffee shop that they sighted Dudamel having a quiet cup of coffee prior to his rehearsal. Nick approached tentatively. 'Maestro, we are so sorry to bother you, but your name is legend in our household and Walter and Sari so wanted to meet you'.

'Hello Walter, nice to meet you, do you play an instrument?'

'Oh yes, I play the ukulele.'

Simón Bolívar Youth Orchestra / Dudamel Conducting

Sonia Baldock

B.Mus (Hons), M.Mus.
MNSc., Grad Cert. Clinical Nursing (Intensive Care)

Critical Nurse Educator, Violin
ADO Concertmaster

'Music is life, it provides nourishment for my soul'

Would you tell us about transitioning from being a professional violinist to becoming an ICU nurse?

I started playing the violin when I was nine years old, but not because I had any desire to play music. We had a very good music teacher at my primary school and it became apparent that I had an affinity for music. There happened to be a violin teacher at my school, so I began violin lessons. The first time that a violin was put into my hands I knew that I would be playing for the rest of my life. I began with a quarter size violin - I'm tiny, I've always been tiny!

My first teacher was Wendy Tooke. I was learning from the Suzuki books, but not the actual method (which usually involves starting at a very early age and learning from ear rather than by reading music). We worked our way through the Suzuki books – mostly I would teach myself pieces well beyond what the class was up to because I was bored. After a year of being in a class with fourteen others I asked if I could do the Australian Music Examination Board (AMEB) exams because I needed the extra push or challenge. By the time I was in high school I was doing my grade 8 AMEB exam and after that I started lessons with William (Bill) Hennessy. I heard him play the Beethoven Violin Concerto and I knew immediately that I wanted to learn from him.

There were two main teachers in Adelaide if you wanted to take music seriously as a career. The choice was between Beryl Kimber and Bill. It was well known that Beryl produced soloists. I knew, even at the age of 13, that if I closed my eyes, I could tell which students learned from her, and those who didn't. I didn't want to sound like everyone else, so I asked Bill if he would teach me. Bill taught me throughout almost my entire Bachelor of Music degree at the University of Adelaide. At the beginning of my Honours year Bill moved to Melbourne to join the Australian National Academy of Music (ANAM). At this point I began lessons with Beryl Kimber.

At the age of nineteen, in my second year of my bachelor's degree, I started working as a casual with the Adelaide Symphony Orchestra (ASO). I knew that if I wanted to take my playing to the next level I would need to travel overseas. I travelled to Germany where I sought lessons with several high-profile violin teachers, in search of "the one". Right at the end of that trip I participated in a short course led by the violinist Zakhar Bron in Vienna, Austria. I played in a couple of master classes with Bron, but I also had four lessons with his assistant, Berent Korfker, an international soloist. I knew quite quickly that I wanted to learn from him.

I came home for a while, saved up, and went back to the Netherlands to study with Berent for one year in 2001. On my return, and after a few more years playing with the ASO, I wanted to live and work somewhere that would provide more challenge, more competition, so I moved to Melbourne. I completed my master's in music performance, learning with Melbourne Symphony Orchestra (MSO) violinist Mark Mogilevski, while also playing in the MSO as a casual player. I played in the MSO for 10 years. Towards the end of that time, I became unwell with an auto immune disease and realised that music was not going to sustain me from a financial point of view if I couldn't land a permanent position with the orchestra.

Could you explain what a casual player is?

A casual orchestral player is employed on a week by week basis. Your wages depend on how many calls you are required to attend each week. (A call is a period of rehearsal or concert up to three hours. So, a rehearsal day of six hours was made up of two calls). A permanent player is on full-time salary. If you are a busy casual, as I was, you could earn quite a good income, but there was no job security. I might be booked up for five weeks in advance, but I never knew what was coming after that.

My transition to nursing is a long and complicated story! I had always been very interested in how the body worked. In the years before leaving music, I had thoughts about doing study about the impact of warm-up stretches prior to practice or performance related injuries. When I made the decision to leave music professionally, I briefly thought about doing medicine. The reason I chose to study nursing instead of medicine was because I had been an inpatient in hospital, and I thought the nurses were absolutely amazing. The doctors would come into the room for only two or three minutes and then they would leave, and I wouldn't see them for the rest of the day! The nurses were always there.

That's because they were seeing other patients and doing clinics. You weren't the only patient they were looking after.

I know, I know, but my nurse was caring for other patients too. I wanted the people contact, the patient contact.

But now you're doing intensive care nursing with people on ventilators that you can't speak to anyway.

Fair point! But you can speak to them and I always do. I didn't actually want to do ICU nursing when I started out for this exact reason. But somehow, I ended up there, and to be perfectly honest, intensive care nursing plays to my type A personality.

How did you feel when you made the transition from being a professional violinist to becoming a nurse.

When I left the MSO and went back to university to start my nursing studies, I quit playing the violin completely. I didn't play for four years apart from the odd wedding or at church. Then I was working as a nurse at Royal Melbourne Hospital (RMH) in the cardiology department. It was my second year out and I had heard about Phillip Antippa's orchestra, Corpus Medicorum.

I happened to run into Phillip in the coffee shop at the hospital. I'm not generally a bold person, but when I saw his name tag, I just went up to him and said, 'Phillip I'm Sonia'. I am an ex-professional violinist and now a nurse here at RMH. I would love to play in your orchestra.'

As a bunch of doctors, you immediately recognised your need for a bossy nurse to join you and take charge! I joined the Australian Doctors Orchestra (ADO) after a couple of years playing with Corpus Medicorum. My first concert with was in Darwin, when I was asked to be the concertmaster.

Playing with ADO is more difficult for me than playing with Corpus because I can't afford the costs of interstate travel as well as the accommodation cost ADO gigs require, whereas Corpus Medicorum always plays right here in Melbourne.

What was your earliest musical recollection?

My music teacher in primary school. We were learning to play the recorder and she noticed that I seemed to understand rhythm, intonation and pitch without effort. She gave me an aural test by playing notes on the piano at random. I was able to sing and tell her what the name of the note was. She told me that I had perfect pitch. After that was when I started to learn the violin. There was no classical music in my family, no one played music on the radio or on records.

Can you remember when music first spoke to you?

When I heard Bill Hennessy play the Beethoven Violin Concerto.

What was your most exciting musical experience as a player and as a listener?

As a listener, it was Gil Shaham playing the Sibelius Violin Concerto with the Adelaide Symphony Orchestra. I was still in high school, and I remember sitting literally on the edge of my seat. I did not sit back, taking in every moment.

I've got a few particularly memorable experiences as a player, the first was when I was playing with the ASO. Vadim Repin, **a Russian soloist,** was playing Shostakovich's first violin concerto. We were doing the dress rehearsal when he played the Cadenza all the way through for the first time……….. The **entire** orchestra forgot to come in at the end of his cadenza because we were all completely floored. Many jaws dropped and we just forgot where we were!

My second memorable moment was in 1998 when we put on the whole of Wagner's Ring cycle in Adelaide. It was the first time it had been done in Australia and it was massive. There were two moments that stood out. One was the opening: we had a water curtain to represent the beginning of time, Genesis. We had been given permission by the fire department to turn off all of the exit lights in order to achieve complete darkness. As an orchestra, we had to memorise the first few minutes of the music, including all the rests. The horns start playing first, and the violins don't come in straight away. There were two metronomes, one either side of the conductor's stand, flashing to show us the beat, and then they turned the lights up, very, very, slowly. Jeffrey Tate conducted the entire cycle from memory.

That was a big experience musically and it was while I was finishing my honours year of my degree. That meant that I had a recital in the middle of playing 'The Ring'. At the end, we received a curtain call and the whole orchestra came up on stage. When the curtains parted there was an enormous roar from the audience. I thought that as classical musician, I'll never experience anything like this again. It was like being at a rock concert.

What does music mean to you?

Music is life, I don't think that the world would be a habitable place without it. It provides nourishment for my soul. In these hard times of Covid, even playing something that's not classical, as in playing with the scrub choir at RMH, it calms my soul. I can't really put it into words. That is probably why I am a violinist, an instrumentalist rather than a singer, writer, or actor, because I don't put things into words easily! I can get lost in music, when I'm playing, the rest of the world just falls away. I've noticed this more as an amateur than when I was playing professionally. The importance now is not how well I play, it is more the importance of just playing incredible music with a bunch of incredible people.

Can you remember when things ever went wrong in a performance?

Plenty of times! We lost the lights in the middle of a concert with the MSO, only the emergency stage lighting left. We were playing Vaughan Williams. We had a hundred extension cords and sconce lights rigged up.

Another time was back in my days with ASO.

We were playing a piano concerto, the soloist was in the middle of his Cadenza, totally engrossed. Sitting there we could hear a fire alarm in the background, which was getting louder and louder. The soloist was so focused that he couldn't hear it. We were starting to look at each other trying to work out what was going on. Eventually, the orchestra manager came on stage and had to tap the pianist on the shoulder to stop.

The entire orchestra and audience were evacuated, until the fire department came and put the fire out. It was real – a small fire in the kitchen. As we were filing back on stage one by one, the orchestra manager stood by the door whispering to each one of us….bar 255….bar 255….. bar 255….. And rather topically for now, as the hospital shook a few weeks ago in a 5.9 magnitude earthquake, I was reminded of a concert I was performing in with the MSO at Hamer Hall. A small tremor caused the stage, which is below sea level, to shake quite noticeably from side-to-side. Not unlike the fire alarm incident, we were all looking at each other wondering if we were the only one feeling this unusual shaking or if everyone else could feel it too.

What are your Desert Island choices?

Heifetz playing the first two Brahms Violin Sonatas and the Franck Sonata - a live recording. There is so much energy and passion because the performance was live. It is obvious that it's not a studio recording. I could listen to that CD over and over. I feel the same about all the Tchaikovsky string quartets and the sextet. I call them 'my happy music' because it doesn't matter what sort of mood I'm in, when I hear them, I feel happy. If I'm already happy, then it makes me even happier. If I'm depressed, it makes me happy. If I'm angry, it makes me happy.

I would also include the Bach cello suites. They are my calming music. I don't like long haul flights. I understand the physics of flight, but I just don't understand how planes can stay up there for so long, so

I can't sleep, I can't do anything, so I listen to Bach while everyone else is fast asleep around me. There's a million more.

I'd like to add my feelings about the transition from music to nursing.

The short answer is, I have never looked back, I've never regretted my decision to quit playing music professionally. I had lost the love a little bit towards the end of my career without realizing, because it was all about performing, all about trying to impress so that I could win a permanent job or win more work. I also had to do a lot of what I would call soul destroying gigs, like playing in the background for a big fancy dinner of high rollers at the casino. It paid well, but this wasn't what I played violin for. It shouldn't be about doing any gig just to pay the rent. It should be playing for love. Playing music had become a job.

When I picked it up my violin again for the first time at the first Corpus concert that I played in, I realised that I had indeed lost the previous love of music that I once had. My love of music, and the violin, has returned, but in a very different and probably more important way. So no, I have never regretted my decision to leave because the moment that I picked up the violin at the age of nine and thought 'I'm going to be doing this for the rest of my life', I **am** still doing it for the rest of my life, just that it's for love rather than money and recognition.

Occasionally, I take my violin to the ICU, and I play for patients. The staff also get as much out of it as the patients. I've been doing that for a few years now, especially when you find someone that just needs that something extra.

That's wonderful.

I play them a variety of pieces. At Christmas I play carols and at other times it could be Bach. Elgar works nicely, as do some other short pieces, and anything baroque usually works well.

Dr Janis Svilans

MBBS FANZCA

Anaesthetist, Cellist

'When the instrument becomes part of you... your body plays'

What's your earliest musical recollection?

Somebody practising the piano at home: it would've been one of my older sisters. I grew up as one of eight. My parents were Latvian refugee migrants, and they were certainly not well off. Despite that, one of the top priorities was to get a piano because my mother had been a piano and singing teacher. We were all put through the mill of learning to play the piano. There was always the radio as well, first thing in the morning ABC radio 5AN, so there was always music at home.

My father played the clarinet in the school orchestra, but he didn't pursue it. My grandfather made his own violin and entertained people at parties by playing Latvian folk music. Legend goes that when he played his violin people's feet had to move so I think there's got to be a musical gene somewhere along the line.

All eight of us were made to play the piano initially. I was never any good on the piano, basically I hated it. I always wanted to play the clarinet. What inspired me was hearing Schubert's "Shepherd and Rock" for soprano, piano and clarinet. Anyway, my mum took me to Gábor Reves, who was the main clarinet person in Adelaide. I was about eight and Gábor looked at me and said, "You're too young, you'll have to wait till you're 12 to start the clarinet". I am pretty sure he was Hungarian.

My mother's friend wanted to get a Latvian string orchestra together and she needed cellos. My mother asked, "Look, do you want to play the cello NOW or wait until you're 12 to play the clarinet?" I was desperate to be done with the piano, so that's how I got onto the cello. My mother's friend's orchestra was called the "Silver Strings". The stars in it were the Larsen twins, Gunars and Mairita, both violinists.

Music has always been very strong in Latvia so it's no surprise that tradition continued here in Adelaide, we had a very active Latvian youth music group. We had a concert every year where everybody was expected to get on stage and perform from memory, it was the most dreadful experience. I remember playing Saint-Saëns's "Allegro Appassionato" which was something I had been working on the previous year.

I started formal lessons initially with David Bishop for a very short time, then moved to James Whitehead. Both teachers taught at the Con. I was an external student there.

I did the AMEB (Australian Music Examinations Board) course to grade seven. By then I had already decided to get into Medicine, so there was no point doing any more AMEB exams. Realistically my decision to do medicine as opposed to Music boiled down to financial security, that's all. I grew up in circumstances where at best we were struggling. Starting a new life in a strange country with a big family was no joke in those days, it may be easier now. The priority was always to have a secure form of employment and medicine could provide that.

I had a stroke of luck and managed to get a job as a casual cellist with the ASO (Adelaide Symphony Orchestra) while I was studying Medicine, that was a great help. I had an audition, which was very informal. It was at when cellist Janis Laurs was playing in the orchestra, he was preparing to go to Switzerland to study with Pierre Fournier. So, a vacancy arose. Janis whispered a few words of recommendation to management even though I had never studied with him. My previous contact with Janis was when we were studying with James Whitehead, my lessons preceded his. While Janis was unpacking his cello I said to James "Who is the best cellist in the world? "He replied "Janis Laurs is the best cellist in the world, and you are second best. 'Well, how could I be second best? I had to do Medicine.'

I continued playing in the conservatorium orchestra during the earlier medical student years and when internship came it completely killed off playing for me, my cello laid dormant for 20 years. Intern year was followed by specialisation, family, mortgages and school fees and a very busy private practice which completely swallowed up my life. Then a former Psychiatry colleague of mine forced me to join a scratch orchestra which he was getting together for a psychiatrists' conference. Since I'd been practising for two weeks for that, I thought I'll play on for another two weeks, so he really got me going. Slowly everything started coming back and I had a few lessons with Ted Brown, the cellist in the former ASQ (Australian String Quartet). Then there were other opportunities like joining community orchestras. Then I heard about ADO. The first one I played in was 2001 in Brisbane, with Peter Tanfield as our soloist playing the Mendelssohn violin concerto.

Playing in ADO for the first time was absolutely fabulous, the whole concept struck a chord with me. I thought this is it, this is a find and I've been to virtually every ADO since then. ADO has become my year's priority and as I look back over the years and think, oh yes, 2010, that was Adelaide, my life is measured by past ADO performances.

When did music first speak to you?

Hearing "Shepherd on the Rock "as we mentioned before, I was 5.

What was your most exciting musical experience as a player and as a listener?

That should have been a question on notice! There are so many. As a performer and as ADO goes, the Saint-Saëns Organ Symphony we performed in Sydney for our 10th anniversary concert was a definite pinnacle. You could feel the organ vibrate in your chest before the sound arrived. You can't have that kind of sensation listening to a recording, your body cavities vibrating.

As a listener, I would say Maxim Vengerov's recital held in the Adelaide Festival Theatre in 2015, I was absolutely spellbound by his playing, all the pieces, including the encores. Often after a concert you think, "Oh, that was the best" till you hear another concert and then you say, "No, maybe that was the best".

What does music mean to you?

Music is something spiritual, definitely, it is a chance for you to express something about your soul through an instrument. Traditionally people have done that by singing, their voice being their instrument. When the instrument becomes part of you, the instrument and you are one, you don't have to think and let your body do the playing. It's a fantastic experience when that happens.

Can you remember an incident where something went wrong in a performance?

Lots of times. The usual thing is losing your place, or the ensemble falling apart. There's been nothing that's been embarrassing, and I've always regarded things going wrong as valuable learning experiences. There is always a reason, and when you learn from it, you become a better player. You can make a complete fool of yourself, but that's not the worst thing in the world, is it?

What would be your desert island music choices?

It would have to be the top five, Beethoven, Mozart, Bach, Brahms and Tchaikovsky.

For me, Beethoven has something special that puts him head and shoulders above the others. Maybe the depth of his personality and his soul, it's hard to define, you don't have to put it into words because it's there in the music. Some of the sublime moments in his Missa Solemnis still bring tears to my eyes. I can't remember the bar number, but there's a fortissimo in the last movement where everyone is going hammer and tongs and then there's a GP (General Pause), basically a triple pianissimo, then the choir comes in very softly. That's magical, but then again, in the Emperor Piano Concerto when the soloist enters, it's a gem, then it's transformed in the subsequent movements. There are so many gems that I wouldn't survive on a desert island, and I would need more.

How much do you practise?

It varies a great deal; on a good day I'd get about two to three hours done and that's enough to wear me out.

Are you target orientated as in practising for a performance or do you discipline yourself to just do exercises and the like?

At the moment the target is being able to front up for my lesson on Mondays and show my teacher that I've actually done something and that my playing is different from the previous Monday. I started taking lessons last December again with Greg Tüske, who is a Hungarian. He spent quite a bit of time in Europe, mostly in Hungary studying and playing with various ensembles and then he returned to Adelaide. It's been very difficult for him to progress his career with COVID. The benefit is mutual, I am sure that he can do with an extra pupil and it's really been fabulous for me to discover many new aspects of playing cello.

You have a great passion for owning several different cellos and you have been philanthropic as regards musicians and the cello community at large. Could you tell me a little about how many cellos you have and which one you are playing at the moment?

At the moment I only have two. At the first Adelaide cello festival in 2008 an instrument was made during the festival by 10 collaborative luthiers. It was already lined up for sale in France. I thought, look, that can't happen, it's the first Adelaide cello festival and it has to stay in Adelaide.

I was going to buy myself an Audi RS 4. "Hey, I could get this cello and buy a VW Golf instead".

The instrument stayed in Adelaide and was played by different cellists until Gemma Phillips purchased it for her use in the ASO.

You sold it for less than what you paid for it?

Just the idea that being a significant instrument, it had to stay here.

What's the greatest number of cellos you've owned at any one time?

Only five. I'd see a cello and think that would be really nice to have and I would just get it. I knew that was crazy. The one I'm playing now was made by Ben Puglisi who runs the Bass Shop in Melbourne, I saw just before the cello festival in 2014. I walked into the studio where they were working on the festival cello and I saw one of the instruments in his shop and said, "Gee, someone's done a wonderful job of restoring that old cello". Ben said, "Oh no, I just finished it last week." Made from a very rare, beautiful birds eye maple for the ribs and back, so then I said, "I'll buy it". A cellist friend said that the instruments had a dead sound, I replied "Yes but it's so beautiful. "Now that it's played in, it has turned into the best instrument I've ever owned. So, don't judge a cello by its appearance nor its early unplayed young sound.

My other cello that I have hung on to is called "The Sleeping Beauty", I picked up in Latvia. There is a haunting story that goes with its purchase. A bit of spookiness about because the official manufacture date on the label inside the back is the 1st. of August 2005, which is my father's death date. Actually my father passed away four years before that. On a previous trip to Latvia, shortly after his passing I had an overwhelming feeling that he was going to find a cello for me. Sure enough, I walked into this music store and there was this cello hanging in the shop and I bought it. Nice, but not great. Then on a subsequent trip, it was my mother's idea for me to get a better instrument, but to make it seem like it was from my dad,  she had a label put inside with my dad's death date written on it, but this is all crazy stuff, sometimes crazy things don't harm anyone, and they make a good story.

When I was buying this cello, it was a bit like being in Singapore where you make an offer and a counteroffer, barter back and forth, the upshot of it was that I said, "Look, I can't afford your asking price "I just haven't got enough money." Overnight I managed to scratch together a few euros and a few American dollars, and I rocked up the next morning, I emptied out all my pockets and put all the cash on the bench in front of the dealer and said, "That's all I've got, take it or leave it." There were 11,000 euros in all, he was asking 15,000 so there was a considerable gap. He sensed that it was either that or no sale and cash is always tempting. They love cash in Latvia.

Would you like to mention anything else?

I never imagined chamber music would become my number one obsession and I have chamber music opportunities here in Adelaide. Nothing that's been stable or ongoing as yet but it's something to work on. I've given up my day job now and I've got all the time in the world. The other bonus is having my place in Cape Jervis where I've already had a few wonderful chamber music weekends and hope that this will be something that will continue. I would very much like to see you there.

Rick McQueen-Thomson

MBBS, FACRRM, Dip.Obst.RCOG.
Dip.Obs.ANZCOG (Adv.), B.Eng.

General Practitioner
Trumpet, Cello

'I play in five orchestras and sing in three choirs. I just love it.'

What was your earliest musical recollection?

I was about three or four when I got enthralled with the song 'Buttons and Bows' from Paleface. It drove my parents mad as I was listening to it all the time. The next thing I remember was the 'cuckoo waltz'. Then I got involved in music, both at school singing and then learning the trumpet aged 10.

I started learning the piano at school when I was about six. My mother bought me a very good quality trumpet when I showed interest in playing. It's a Besson 10-10 which I still have. My mother was very musical, she could sing and play the piano. My sister is a very good pianist and she still plays.

I had lessons on the trumpet but unfortunately my first teacher was a pianist who knew very little about the trumpet. Eventually, I was taught by Stan Roberts, who was a member of the MSO, I was about 14 then.

What was your most exciting music you experienced as a player and as a listener?

Playing in a brass band at school, I particularly enjoyed playing a piece called 'The Falcon'. Unfortunately, we only played it for one year and then never played it again. Then I attended the national music camp as a trumpeter and after that I was really hooked. We played César Franck's Symphony in D and Tchaikovsky's Symphony Number Five

Did you have any other memorable experiences as a trumpeter?

Chris Martin was conducting Dvorak's Symphony No 8. In the fourth movement, there is a trumpet call. Every time at rehearsal I stuffed it up, but then in the performance I relaxed, sat back and played it perfectly. Anne (Rick's wife) was in the Bass section sitting with a psychiatrist friend. Anne was quite tense about my solo, the psychiatrist noticed this, after my solo he turned to her and said, 'Oh, you can relax now he got it'.

The next episode was after I had stopped playing trumpet and changed to the cello. We were rehearsing the Grieg piano concerto. We reached a big trumpet solo in the piece but by now I was a cellist, and there was dead silence as I hadn't been replaced. Chris was totally bewildered by what happened because he thought I was still playing trumpet.

What made you change from trumpet to cello?

Mainly because I lost a lot of my teeth through gum disease, and I just couldn't play the trumpet anymore. It was really sad actually, because I had reached a good standard and had mastered that very high piccolo trumpet part in Bach's second Brandenburg Concerto. That part is a Mount Everest for trumpeters. I thought, well, I don't want to give music up so picked up the cello, I was in my fifties. I had never played a string instrument before. The transition took me a while and I worked hard at it. I am about to do my grade eight cello exam and hope to do my A.Mus.A after that.

As a listener I love Prokofiev's 'Peter and the Wolf' especially the sound of the four horns playing the wolf. It sends a shiver up my spine every time I hear it as does hearing Tchaikovsky's 'Waltz of the Flowers'.

As a listener I also love Carl Orff's 'Carmina Burana'. I had a record of it which I totally wore out. Then I got a chance to sing it, and as I lived in the country, I joined the Wangaratta Choir. My son told me he was coming up from Melbourne to sing with this country choir. My reply was 'Snap, I'm the country choir'. There was an ophthalmologist from Albury who sang with me. I sang with the University of Melbourne Choir for quite some time. I also sang in various musicals in places where I had worked in the country and when I eventually started coming down to Melbourne in 1996, I joined an orchestra and joined another choir.

What sort of access is there in the country to pursue music?

My wife was very keen to get our kids playing so she organised, through the Arts Council, a music program in Deniliquin in which tutors came up from the VCA and taught the kids. We held several music camps throughout the year, allowing the kids to play together. It was a very successful program, and is still running. She got a thank-you certificate from the New South Wales government, in recognition of her work. Personally, access was very difficult, so I joined the school orchestra in Finley which was just starting up. She got me into the orchestra and that allowed me to reach my previous level of trumpet playing.

What does music mean to you?

I'd be absolutely devastated if I couldn't keep up my music, I just love it. I love singing, playing in different groups and I am in the process of starting a string quartet, but of course with Covid it's a bit difficult or impossible. I play in five orchestras and sing in three choirs. One of the orchestras, the Victorian Concert Orchestra, travels to the country to give performances. We rehearse for four weeks beforehand. It's a good standard, and we play mostly popular tunes and popular classics. We usually have a singer or two join us. We are picked up by bus and taken to the venues and at the end of the day dropped back again. Depending on how far it is, we sometimes drive ourselves and stay overnight.

How does that ADO come into your life?

I played in the very first concert and most concerts ever since, I've always loved playing with them ever since. The problem for me now, because I'm retired, is that I can't really afford to spend $3,000 or $4,000 when we go interstate.

How did you become aware of ADO?

Victor Karaffa the GP, told me about it. Victor is a good cellist and at our first ADO concert he plunked himself next to the leader in the front desk, thinking it would be all right on the day. As he hadn't practised he realised things would not be OK and quickly took himself to the back of the section.

Can you remember when things went wrong in a performance?

I was playing trumpet in 'Oklahoma', and I could hear that the strings were getting lost. I was counting rigidly, and I knew exactly when the brass were to come in we came in at the right spot, you could see the relief on the conductor's face. He looked much happier after that as the whole thing came together. Another incident was when Chris Martin was demonstrating a point playing with Rowan Thomas's bow. He lost control of the bow which flew over the head of the strings and was luckily caught and wasn't damaged. Rowan's face turned white. I asking

Rowan later how much the bow was worth, who had recovered by then said, 'about $16,000'.

What are your Desert Island discs choices?

Well, I'd obviously like to take my cello. The Bach Cello Suites, I love those. They're really great, what else would I like to take? Benjamin Britten Cello Suites, which I haven't played as yet.

It's difficult because there is so much music I can't live without. César Franck Symphony in D which has great trumpet parts. It also requires some difficult transposing, requiring you to transpose up four and a half notes. Trumpeters learn to transpose at sight. You're happily going along and all of a sudden, you're wondering 'what the hell is the key we are playing in now? Another piece, the Saint-Saens 'Organ Symphony'. Brass players love it. I would also add Shostakovich's Symphony 5 and 10 as well as some baroque music

How much do you practise Rick?

I try to do at least an hour a day. I would like to do more, but I have a whole lot of other things to do. Ideally, I'd like to do four hours a day.

How many days a week are you rehearsing with your orchestras and choirs?

Let's see, Tuesday, Thursday, Saturday, and Sunday. That's four days a week; on Tuesdays and Thursdays I have two rehearsals.

Who are your most significant figures in your musical life?

Chris Martin obviously. I had immense respect for him, he was a terrific conductor and Gerald Keuneman , a fine cellist and also a very good conductor who knows how to deal with adults as well as being a lovely guy. Doug Heywood is a choral director, as well as being a brilliant singer. He knows what he wants from his choir, and he insists on the best.

I am aware of only one other string player besides myself who also sings, her name is Sophie Pewker, who has an absolutely gorgeous contralto voice. I sing bass. I have to add that I am not a soloist, I am a chorister.

Naham Warhaft

MB.BS., FANZCA FACHAM (RACP)

Anaesthetist, Tuba

'Maybe the instrument choice relates to the medical the medical specialty'

What were your earliest musical recollections and how did you arrive at playing the tuba?

I was forced to learn piano as a small child, and I had very little natural ability. I resisted having to practise, all in all I was a difficult pupil, but my parents insisted that I persist for at least a few years. That went on until I reached Melbourne High School. It was in the first week at Melbourne High, that I learned they were forming a new school brass band and were looking for anyone who was interested in joining. I said, 'Absolutely, I'd love to be playing in the band.

The band master was a wonderful bloke, Bob Dunn. He presented me with a tenor horn. Taking it home I said, 'Mum and Dad, I'm going to play this in the band, and I want to stop my piano lessons'. The great thing about the piano lessons was that I could read music. I had that advantage over the other kids. After about three months of the tenor horn, I realised that it was the viola of the brass band. It seemed to me that it was a go-nowhere instrument, it doesn't have a great repertoire outside brass ensembles.

I was also conscious of the fact that there were two instruments in the band that were very versatile. You could play them in symphony orchestras, brass bands, concert bands jazz bands. Those two instruments were the trumpet and the trombone, but I was stuck with the tenor horn.

I heard there was a bass trombone lying in the store and nobody had taken it up. The only brass band instrument that is written for bass clef. All the other brass band instruments are written in treble clef, including the tubas and they need to transpose. I still don't know to this day why, it is written in the bass clef, with no need to transpose.

I don't think anyone else knew bass clef. So, I went to the band master and said, 'Sir, I can read bass clef, and there's a bass trombone in the storeroom. Would you mind if I switch to it? He agreed and that started me off on the lower brass. I played the bass trombone for the next two and a half years.

When we got to Matriculation, all the tuba players who were all the big kids because we were a marching band graduated. So, there were no tuba players. I was five feet 10 in those days and was asked if I could transfer to the tuba, I reluctantly agreed. I enjoyed the bass trombone, but the tuba suited me better because I don't believe I have much natural ability as a musician. Also, I would certainly not be the person you would turn to for tuning an instrument. The bass trombone is rather like a violin in that you make your own notes, whereas the tuba is a valve instrument, and the notes are determined by the exact length of the tubing that is introduced with each valve, so it suited me very well from a tuning point of view.

Realising that it could be played in a symphony orchestra was a huge plus. Same goes for the bass trombone but I figured there'd be less competition for tuba players. About halfway through my matriculation year I was summoned to the principal's office, still in my first year on the tuba. An eminent educationalist, our principal Brigadier George Langley, loved and nurtured our brass band.

He said, 'Warhaft, why aren't you doing matriculation music as a subject?' As I wanted to be a doctor, I was doing physics, chemistry, biology, and science. I replied 'There are two reasons, first of all, this is my first year on the tuba and secondly, there is no syllabus for the tuba in the matriculation handbook.

Leafing through the handbook in his office, he looked it up and said, 'Yes it's true'. The trumpet, trombone, French horn, and the whole woodwind family of instruments were listed but not the tuba.

'We'll fix that'. A couple of weeks went by, and he called me back, 'I've just been talking to the principal trumpet in the MSO, Merv Simpson, and I explained the problem to him. I've arranged for you to go to his house in Oakleigh and we will get a matriculation syllabus together for the tuba.' He did this. It was pretty standard and was based on other brass instruments. It included major and minor scales in all keys as well as the usual test pieces. It was my first music exam of any kind.

Four or five months later, I went along to the examination at the Conservatorium. My examiner was Squadron Leader Hicks, who had a reputation as a very, very difficult examiner. He started me off by asking me to play a scale. I played -one octave - and he said 'please do two octaves. I responded, 'Sir, the syllabus says one octave for all scales. Then there was a bit of a dispute between him and my piano accompanist, who was a lovely guy. It was settled in my favour, the long and the short of it was that I passed matriculation tuba. As far as I knew I was the first person in Australia to achieve that and I was quite proud of myself.

Next year (1956) I started Medicine and like so many school brass-players I dropped playing completely. In my second year of Medicine a close friend, a bassoon player alerted me to the Australian Music Camp held every year at Mittagong. 'Why don't you come along?' About six months later, the first Australian Youth Orchestra was formed. It was 1957 and Sir Bernard Heinze was conducting. The concert was held at the Sydney Town Hall, and I got the guernsey as the tuba player. There was almost nothing on the repertoire for tuba other than the national anthem. I got on the train; we were billeted, and I had a wonderful week. On about the second or third day of rehearsal I got a call to Heinze's office and terrified, I walked in unsure what this was all about. He said, 'Look, the Beethoven Fifth that we're playing, we're very, very short on double basses, could you double up on the double bass parts on your tuba?'

I looked at him with astonishment and said, 'I'll do what I can, but please don't expect much.' In the scherzo the double bass part is fiendish and was way beyond my pay grade. All the same, it was my introduction to a proper orchestra and that was great. I played with the AYO for several years and thoroughly enjoyed it.

When I graduated as a doctor, again I dropped the tuba and music altogether for a couple of decades. One day I was sitting at home and a thought came across my mind, 'Why don't I buy a tuba and have a few lessons?' So, I did. I started playing again, and that brings me up to the Australian Doctors Orchestra, it was 1995.

I was the duty emergency anaesthetist and on a Wednesday morning at Box Hill Hospital I was sitting in the doctors' lounge, I picked up a copy of the Medical Journal of Australia and there was an article by your good self about this orchestra called the Australian Doctors Orchestra and that's when I contacted you. That was my entry into playing with ADO.

Have you done any of the AMEB exams?

I hadn't done any AMEB exams, but I got into the Australia Youth Orchestra, for two reasons, firstly, I had my matriculation, which meant I had reached about 7th grade AMEB level, which was the qualification that they wanted and secondly, and probably more importantly, there weren't many tuba players around, certainly not many orchestral ones.

This was before the big upsurge in brass-music education in schools. Very few schools had brass bands or brass teachers like Melbourne High, Scotch and Melbourne Grammar - no more than a half a dozen or so. These days practically all high schools have a brass band. The people that did play tuba, and some of them were much, much better than me, didn't realise it was an orchestral instrument. To them it was just a brass band instrument like a tenor or flugel horn. So, there was no competition, I think that's really important to understand. These days, there would be 50 tuba players in schools across Melbourne who are all better than I am.

Just let me get this straight, you were in the school band firstly playing tenor horn, then bass trombone and finally the tuba. Did you play in any other bands or orchestras?

When I left school, I had a few months' association with the Caulfield Citizens' Band. I dropped it altogether, but around the mid 1980's I joined the Eltham Concert Band, which was quite a good suburban musical group. Run by Ernie Shade, who was very well known in musical circles, and father of Fred Shade who played piccolo in the Melbourne Symphony Orchestra. I played with them for about 10 or 15 years. In 1997 I joined the Malvern Citizens Band, now called the Stonnington Brass and I've been with them ever since.

What were your impressions of ADO when you first joined us in Sydney in 1995?

I had never played in an orchestra of such a high standard. I thought it was a privilege to be playing with a talented group of people. At the after-party I ran into a piano teacher by the name of Nahamah Patkin - well-known in musical circles in Melbourne for introducing the Yamaha Piano Method into schools. She said, 'Naham, that is the very best non-professional orchestra I've ever heard. I thought, 'How lucky am I to be involved in this.' I continued to play with ADO for 15 years. It gave me the opportunity to play in all state capitals except Perth and Darwin, I've played under some wonderful conductors and alongside really gifted musicians.

What was your most exciting musical experience as a player and as a listener?

As a player, a highlight was Wagner's Meistersingers Overture in Sydney with the Australian Youth Orchestra. It is one of the few orchestral pieces that has a tuba solo. It's a beautiful melody and a lovely work to play, but it's got one tricky note, a top E Natural which is quite a challenge to play. I think I got it right and I felt quite good about it. At the interval, I was sitting backstage having a cup of tea. and this six foot four, very well-built, big man, came up to me and said, 'my name is Cliff Goodchild, I play the tuba in the Sydney Symphony Orchestra and I'd just like to shake your hand and thank you for a job well done.'

That started a relationship with Cliff, a wonderful human being as well as a wonderful tuba player. That was the most memorable individual moment, but I've had thrilling experiences playing music since then.

As a listener, hearing the trumpets, drums and chorus in the second part of the Verdi Requiem always makes my blood run cold, it's just a wonderful thing. I love Verdi, I love opera, but particularly the Requiem.

What does music mean to you?

Music is my major hobby, it's been my main interest outside family and work, I still enjoy playing in the U3A Symphony Orchestra (which I joined 16 years ago) and until recently, two brass bands. (I was a member of Whitehorse Brass Band from 2014 until 2020). I love jazz too and from 2005, till Covid I played the sousaphone in a trad-jazz band.

Is the sousaphone the same as a tuba?

It's the same, it just has a very large bell, it's a tuba that you climb into.

Can you remember when things went wrong in a performance?

Oh yes! Most recently I fluffed a solo bit with one of the brass bands that I play with. Like any musician, I've experienced times where I, or my section or some other section of the orchestra came unstuck for a moment or two, but that's to be expected.

What are your Desert Island choices of music?

I'd take some opera, a selection of Verdi. Recently I saw a performance of Gounod's Faust which I thoroughly enjoyed. I love American musicals such as South Pacific, Guys and Dolls, Oklahoma and My Fair Lady which come to mind. That sort of stuff, I just love it. I saw a performance of Oklahoma done by a Melbourne high school a few years ago and it brought tears to my eyes.

How much do you practise?

Not a lot, especially with Covid, I practise if there is something to practise for, such as an upcoming concert.

Who were the musically significant people in your life?

Definitely Bob Dunn. About eight years ago, we got together as an old Melbourne High School boys' band. We played at a couple of High

School anniversaries. I got it together and we called it the 'Bob Dunn Band.'

In terms of orchestral playing, Chris Martin was wonderful to play under. As well as ADO he also conducted the U3A orchestra with which I still play.

There's an Australian Doctors Orchestra research project in the making for somebody - to relate the instruments people play to the profession they hold within medicine. If you look at the brass players as a group, they tend to be proceduralists, anaesthetists and surgeons, on the other hand if you look at the string players, they tend to be GP's, psychiatrists and physicians, the touchy feely people.

Dr Philip Griffin

MB,BS.,FRACS

Plastic Surgeon, Viola

'I routinely play whilst operating. Music acts as a soothing overlay'

What are your earliest musical recollections and your journey to playing the viola?

As a child there wasn't that much music in our house. My parents would listen to the radio which was always tuned to the ABC and it often featured Peter Dawson, the very successful Australian (Adelaide) bass-baritone. My father was an electrical engineer, a Senior Lecturer at the University of Adelaide. We travelled for a year on his first sabbatical appointment to Cornell University, in Ithaca, upstate New York. I was nine years old, and I found myself going to a school where music tuition was free. The thought of playing a musical instrument hadn't entered my thoughts till then.

I was the middle one of five boys and my mother said, 'Would you like to learn a musical instrument?' I replied, yes. Then she asked, 'What would you like to play?' Because we visited a family whose son was playing the French horn, I said, 'French horn'. She said, 'You mean the Viola?'

'Is that like a French horn?'

'Well, it's a little bit like one.'

When the viola arrived, it was a bit of a surprise, but it was a great start, really. Choosing the viola for me showed a remarkable degree of insightfulness on her part because I was a bit old starting to play at 9-10 years of age. When you join an orchestra, you don't need to be at the same standard as a violinist, Viola parts are not as demanding.

Being a competitive chap, and seeing all these seven year old girls playing better than me in the orchestras motivated me to get up to speed. We were only away for one year and when we came back to Adelaide we found a local teacher, that worked out very well.

I was passed to Jean Monro, who was the viola leader in the Adelaide Symphony Orchestra (ASO) as she was doing a little bit of teaching at the Flinders Street School of Music. Subsequently I learnt from Richard Hornung who took me through to the finals. I said, 'look, I'm not doing enough practice' I was in third or fourth year medicine at this stage. It's not making these lessons worth your while. He said, 'Well Phil, it's always good to have two alternatives, I'm not so sure about this medicine business.' 'If I worked really hard, where do you see me going?', 'Well, you might get a role with the Tasmanian Symphony.' which was not at the standard it is now. That's what I thought, because I don't have perfect pitch and my musical memory is not all that great. These are things you need to be a professional musician; it's just taken as standard.

I did the first five AMEB exams but the shortcomings of not having aural skills meant that the theory side of it was too tricky for me. As the pieces became more difficult it kept on being a challenge. I probably would have been able to do the higher technical grades, seven, and eight, with a push.

Did you play in orchestras after that?

The whole thing about playing an orchestral instrument is actually the orchestra. As an adolescent, if playing an instrument answers your emotional needs, then you'll keep going, at least that was true for me. You can expect some teasing at school, but they stop when you point out that there are more girls in an orchestra than in a football team.

Medical studies are challenging and the time required to succeed in surgical training, in my case Plastic and Reconstructive Surgery, is overwhelming. Fortunately, my wife is a beautiful violinist, and so I was able to keep a trickle of musical activity going, with a string quartet, and occasional piano quartet meetings.

Just before my surgical fellowship exam we were in Glasgow for a year of Plastic Surgery training. My wife found the amateur music opportunities there were fantastic! She was playing with the "The Glasgow Symphony Orchestra". I joined them for my first Shostakovich symphony, a terrific experience. In fact, the music in Scotland was fantastic, if it wasn't for the weather, we probably could have stayed there.

The next year we were in Louisville, Kentucky, for a Hand Surgery Fellowship. Music opportunities there were the diametric opposite. The music there was either Country or Western. In their defence, they did have a Symphony Orchestra, but very sparse amateur opportunities.

On our return to Adelaide, I hadn't rejoined our local community orchestra, The Burnside Symphony. In fact, the Australian Doctors Orchestra gave me the initiative to start playing again. That was actually entirely to do with meeting you. We were sitting in an airport waiting, after a plastic surgery meeting, and when you found out that I played the viola you encouraged me to join ADO and so my first concert was in 1994.

Do you play much chamber music?

Together with my wife, we formed a string quartet with friends and played together for more than 10 years. We covered a lot of repertoires, extended to Piano Quartets and Quintets but eventually met less frequently, and stopped.

Dr Philip Griffin

Can you remember when music first spoke to you?

One of the big revelations for me as a boy was playing at the Adelaide May Music Camp sharing the section front desk with Patricia Pollett[4], who became a very fine professional violist. A string quartet from the ASO gave a lunchtime recital. They performed Schubert's 'Death and the Maiden' quartet in D minor. I had not heard a string quartet before, it was lyrical poetry, it was a revelation.

That meant something, the sonority of those string instruments playing together as well as the musical communication was unforgettable, I was 15.

What has been your most exciting musical experience as a player and as a listener?

As a listener, hearing Jane Peters playing the Tchaikovsky Violin Concerto with ADO in Adelaide was terrific. Even though I'd been organising the ADO to come to Adelaide, I chose to sit it out for that piece and be in the audience. We needed a smaller orchestra for the concerto, and I could just enjoy the performance. She is a very gifted violinist.

I think most of the big occasions have been with ADO. We've tackled some works which seemed impossible at first, but we made them work. For example, the Hobart concert with the Sibelius violin concerto and Rimsky-Korsakoff's Scheherazade was spectacular. We played at a high standard, really enjoyable for the listeners and as a player I felt very privileged.

---

4   Patricia Pollett is Professor of Viola at University of Queensland

Music Is Medicine

What does music mean to you?

It would be a very, very dull world without the classical music heritage. I routinely play music whilst operating and it served a couple of purposes, you as a surgeon, would really appreciate this, when you concentrate on a particularly difficult technical spot, having people gossiping and doors slamming in the background is distracting. It puzzled me that while the central activity in the theatre is actually what you're doing with your hands and everyone else is meant to be supporting you, but they don't see it that way. Music provides a healing background and if you play pieces that you can actually listen to it helps you to ignore the rest. Those distractions can build up and impair your concentration- and technical performance. Should you have to instruct staff concentration, you can go beyond the limit of irritation into anger and that mucks you up and you lose your focus.

Music acts as a soothing overlay. I did find at least one staff member who took it as a personal insult that I was playing classical music. That gave me a bit of an insight into the rich tapestry of everyone's childhood and the baggage we all carry.

Can you remember when things went wrong in a performance?

That would be my very first orchestral performance. I was an earnest viola player- the only one in the high school orchestra. My part was specially written out for the viola, it was by the Beatles called 'Yesterday.' I was earnestly playing pizzicato (plucking the string) at the beginning of each bar when after about 15 bars, I realised that nobody else was playing, the orchestra had all (except me) stopped! Someone near me had to dig me in the ribs to stop me, that was a pretty bad one. Clearly, I hadn't been watching the conductor since the beginning of the piece.

I don't think ADO has ever ground to a complete halt but there certainly have been some rocky bits.

Despite that we've had some amazing performances. Take our performance in Canberra of the Rachmaninov 'Variations on a Theme by Paganini' played by Clemens Leske. He had influenza and had been in bed with the fever and then just came out and played spectacularly well; professional musicians have an enormous depth of commitment.

What are your desert island choices?

Oh, how many do you get? Dvorak is such a great composer for the viola and also his orchestration superb. His string quartet 'The American' is a total highlight, I would have to have that. Then Bach's 'Chaconne', for solo violin, it has so much complexity, Mozart's, 'Ave Verum Corpus', that's just beautiful music, very beautiful. Those are three pieces that I'd have to have with me. There are many more. I've come to appreciate Vaughan Williams more since we played his 'London' symphony with ADO.

How much do you play?

The pandemic has caused a bit of a stop, but I really hope that by 2022, we will be able to play as an orchestra again. I don't know how we could remove the power from the chief medical officers, some of them are kind of enjoying it.

Did your parents play an instrument?

My mother revealed that she had always wanted to play the violin, but she didn't. She had sisters playing the piano, it was a big family, and the money didn't stretch to her and she took that on board.

Do any of your siblings play?

My younger brother learned the violin for a while and the youngest, the cello but it didn't really stick with them, they gave it up.

And your children?

The oldest plays violin, not so much at the moment, but she was playing there in Melbourne, the next plays some piano, the youngest, plays cello and I'm looking at his cello here as we speak. He's in Perth, but his cello is here, he hasn't played it for years. It's a pity that he didn't keep going, he had something.

Dr. Rachel Lind

MB.ChB, FACEM

Emergency Physician, Cello

'Music Means Joy: it's shaped me as a person'

What are your earliest music recollections and how did you arrive at playing the cello?

I've always loved music ,thanks to my mum, there was always a lot of singing in the car and listening to, and watching, things like 'The Sound of Music'. I'd watch this every time I visited with my grandma. I was born in Aberdeen, Scotland. I participated in the school music curriculum in my earliest school years. We were all made to play the recorder (every parent's worst nightmare) and I sang in the choir. At some stage we were assessed as to whether we should learn a musical instrument or not. I remember, aged seven, first meeting my cello teacher – Hilary Cromar – when she came into my classroom saying, 'Can Rachel Lind please come with me'. I obviously had a guilty conscience because I assumed that I was being taken to the headmaster's office for a telling off. Instead, she took me to the music room and showed me this rather large looking violin-shaped instrument and said, 'This is a cello, would you like to learn to play it?' and I said, 'Yeah, all right'.

As it turns out, I took to it naturally and was reasonably good at it. I studied with Hilary for the rest of my school years and also began monthly lessons with a visiting Professor from the London Colleges, James Halsey, when I was fourteen.

My first exposure to orchestral playing was a couple of years in when I started attending the local music centre in Aberdeen on Saturday mornings. This was a council-run music initiative for all school-aged kids in the area, run by the local music teachers. There were ensembles for all abilities starting with "Initial Strings' for the very beginners scratching away on violins learning to play together, all the way through to the senior ensembles.

There were string orchestras, concert bands for the brass and woodwinds and the big one was the senior symphony orchestra. These met weekly during term time and would culminate with concerts at Christmas and Easter.

Through the Aberdeen Music Centre I became involved in a wonderful chamber group run by a violin teacher, the late Malcolm Bolton, 'The Aberdeen Youth String Ensemble', or AYSE. Whilst it was a requirement for all the teachers to run these groups, I think perhaps for some it was just one of those things that they had to do as part of their job. Mr B. was not one of those, he was passionate about music and mentored us in the nuances of ensemble playing, and interpretation of mainly baroque and early classical music like Handel's Concerto Grossos but also in lesser-known later works such as Gerald Finzi's Dies Natalis and Arvo Part's Summa. He really encouraged us and as a result we not only played the standard end of term concerts, but also gave regular charity concerts in church halls and the local Art Gallery and we were even selected to take part in the National Festival of Music for Youth competition at South Bank Centre in London in 2003. This was a hugely positive influence during my teen years and taught me to develop a real love for a much broader range of music.

I was also lucky enough to be selected to play in the National Youth Orchestras of Scotland (NYOS) from age 11, initially with their junior orchestra (then the National Children's Orchestra of Scotland) and from 13 with the senior orchestra (the National Youth Orchestra of Scotland) which had a biannual intensive residential format leading to a concert tour similar to AYO. I toured with them several times to halls in the UK and Europe and got to work with seasoned conductors like Sian Edwards and soloists like Janine Jansen and even a very young Nicola Benedetti.

At that point did you want to do Medicine?

Up until fifth year of high school (equivalent to grade 11) I was still determined to do Music. I was going to go to the Royal College of Music, then do a post-grad at Juilliard in Performance. That was the plan. At that stage I had probably been getting by on talent, I put in intermittent bouts of hard work for my cello exams - I did all the ABRSM exams (equivalent of AMEB) and gained Distinction in every one (except Grade One, we don't talk about that) and for Grade Seven I actually got the highest mark in the country - but I didn't sustain it. I hated playing scales and exercises and preferred just to get my teeth into pieces like the Elgar concerto.

Basically, I wasn't putting in the work needed to achieve my full potential. I sat down with James and had a reality check. I could coast along as I was, but I wouldn't have a solo career. I wouldn't even have an orchestral career, as there would be reams of other people who worked hard to achieve that. I decided that I loved music dearly and didn't want to resent it as 'The Job'. I was still getting academically good grades, so I changed tack completely and decided to do something entirely different that involved science and where I could work with people. I applied to Medicine, and I got into Aberdeen University.

For the first few years of uni I played in the university orchestra and I kept playing with NYOS twice a year, as principal cello. Then commitments at university increased and it became harder to fit everything in, so I gave up NYOS after almost ten years with them. After graduation I moved to Edinburgh to work as a junior doctor. I still played in a string quartet there, because that's all I could find time for, but that definitely sparked a love for some of the meatier chamber music works like Shostakovich string quartets.

I moved to Australia in 2011 after working in Edinburgh for two years. I was still very much a baby doctor. Initially, I was in Townsville, Queensland and I didn't bring my cello with me, as I thought I'd only be away for a year, and thought maybe I could hire one. Shortly after arriving I discovered the local community orchestra, 'The Barrier Reef Orchestra'. I managed to borrow a cello from a local teacher for one concert but soon realised I wouldn't be able to hire one in Townsville. I don't think there was even a music shop, so I went down to Brisbane and bought a cello.

I had been playing with BRO for a couple of years when I started hearing rumours about a doctors' orchestra. I eventually found out the details, applied, and so my first concert with ADO was in Geelong, in regional Victoria in 2014. I couldn't have even told you where Geelong was on the map before this so this was a great experience to see a bit of regional Australia! It was one of Warwick Stengårds's first concerts and we played a mix of some excerpts from opera arias. I'd been enjoying playing with BRO but there was a limit on how much they could do. ADO had some really good players and I quickly realised that 'this is what I've been missing'.

What I loved about that first encounter with ADO was that when you were networking with people during tea and coffee time, you wouldn't just be asking, 'What do you play?' You'd also ask, 'What medical specialty are you in and where have you come from?'. These were the three standard questions you asked first before you got to know the person better. I just found this really fascinating.

Then I heard a bit of a buzz during one of the coffee breaks where some of the players were talking about an upcoming tour to Russia with another doctors' orchestra, Corpus Medicorum. I thought, 'hang on a minute, THEY ARE GOING ON A TOUR!?'. I knew then I'd found my people. I didn't go on that particular tour with Corpus, but it was probably my impetus for making the move to Melbourne a couple of years later so I could join that orchestra too.

I found the rehearsal format for ADO – an intense 3 days of rehearsals followed by a performance – works really well for someone like me who is a shift worker. It's less of a commitment than trying to fit weekly rehearsals in with my roster, and still creates great results. Corpus Medicorum works the same way more or less.

Can you remember when music as such first spoke to you?

Music was always around. Apparently my grandfather on my mother's side, whom I never met, could pick up an instrument and immediately be able to play it. My mother played the piano, but not to a high standard and early on she was my accompanist, but she used to joke that once my pieces got too difficult, she would have to stop.

What was the most exciting musical experience for you as a player and as a listener?

There's been a few! It's hard to choose! My most exciting moment was probably playing in the BBC Proms in the Albert Hall, that was pretty cool. That was with the National Youth Orchestra of Scotland, at the start of our summer European tour. Later we went over to the Schleswig-Holstein Festival and then on to Berlin, with Martyn Brabbins conducting. I remember everybody had a bit of a crush on our soloist Håkan Hardenberger, the Swedish trumpeter. The Proms concert was broadcast live on BBC Radio Three which allowed my grandmother to listen to our performance which was special. It was in 2003 I would have been 17.

Can you remember what pieces you played?

I can't remember what the overture that we did was, but we did play a commissioned trumpet concerto by British composer Sally Beamish, which was actually quite good fun. Part of the piece involved the percussion section playing on things from a scrap yard. The composer actually took a couple of the percussionists to a car-junkyard to pick out things like car-springs and the like, so it was a bit out there, but it was also quite lyrical. We also played Elgar's second symphony.

As a listener one really special memory that stands out for me was when I went to Paris with my mother a few years ago and we stumbled across an evening concert at Saint Chapelle featuring Vivaldi's Four Seasons in the church sanctuary itself. We experienced this lovely concert with beautiful stained-glass windows all around us. It was quite special.

What does music mean to you?

Joy! It's been a really important outlet for me. It provides new challenges and gives me a sense of achievement to this day. It afforded me wonderful experiences that I got to have as part of an orchestra, and I think it really shaped me as a person and actually made me grow up a little bit. It's also formed many friendships. There are some people from my teenage years who I'm still in touch with to this day and it's been a method for networking and making new friends whenever I moved locations. For example, when I moved to Townsville, it was the Barrier Reef Orchestra that helped me make some non-medical friends and the same again when I moved to Melbourne.

Can you remember, um, when things went wrong in a concert?

Oh, a couple of times. (Peals of laughter).

I played with a local semi-professional orchestra in Aberdeen before I finished uni, and one of the regular conductors stuffed up the beginning of Beethoven's Fifth so badly that I thought we were going to have to start again! Whenever I've played it since I've always been anxious about that opening. It's so exposed and everybody knows it, you certainly don't want to be the player who comes in early!

What are your Desert Island disc choices?

The Elgar Cello Concerto is an absolute must, with Jacqueline du Pré playing. Shostakovich Symphony number Five, I think you and I have had this discussion many times about Shosta Five versus Shosta 10, love them both, but Shosta Five does it for me.

When you asked me earlier, "what does music mean to you", it's transporting. For me it links your memories and transports you to a time where you played that piece before and where you were in your life at that time. With Shosta Five I was experiencing my first love, my first boyfriend, a bassoonist who broke my heart. So, I can never really listen to the third movement without being reminded of that, a 15 year old Rachel, who is feeling really sad as the cellos are playing this beautiful melody up in the rafters.

I'd take Rachmaninov's second symphony as well, because it's so beautiful and Brahms String Quartet in C minor because of that juicy cello bit in the first movement. Honestly, there's just too much to choose from, I'll take a whole iPod.

Mary Frost

MB.BS, DRANZRCOG, FRANZCP

Psychiatrist, Viola

'Yeah, my parents loved Wagner and so I became a psychiatrist.'

What's your earliest musical recollection?

My parents listened to a lot of Wagner, so my earliest musical recollection is my parents and some of their friends sitting around a valve radio that my father, who was an electrical engineer, had built. Subsequently, I learned German, and I still remember this phrase from my childhood: "Hier ist der Bayerischer Rundfunk (Bavarian Broadcasting service....)" The announcement was referring to a German broadcast of Wagner from Bayreuth. My parents would be sitting there with librettos, scores, and pencils while they were listening. I must have been about 4 then. I didn't remember the German as a four-year-old, but when I learnt German later as a teenager, it all made sense.

Although my mother didn't have a music degree, she had an arts degree majoring in French, and was an accomplished pianist and repetiteur. That's where my love of chamber music came from. A lot of singers came around to our house. We grew up in Woomera, which was both literally and metaphorically a musical desert, except for our house. My mother was so desperate to play music publicly that she would keep changing her religion. If the Catholics needed an organist, she would be quite happy to be Catholic, if the Protestants needed an accompanist for hymns and carols, she would be Protestant.

We had a piano in the house, the radio was constantly on and tuned to the ABC, and we had old 78 records to play. Although Dad wasn't a musician, he absolutely adored music and was really passionate about it. He brought an intellectual side to music; for instance, he read the Grove Dictionary of Musicians. We had a very stimulating musical household, even though none of us kids could play instruments except for the recorder, as there was no musical program at local the school.

We were in Woomera because my father was a rocket scientist. We lived there until I was ten. Australia was part of the European Launch and Development Organization Program (ELDO) which put a rocket called Blue Streak into the sky. Australia, in fact in the 1950's and 60's the whole Western world believed that the future of Defense lay with rocket technology after the Germans developed the V2's which were so destructive in Europe during WWII. The Brits developed their own rocket program together with the Americans and other European nations. Australia provided a vast country in which to test them. So as kids, we would ask Mum at night:

'Where's daddy?'

'Oh, he's out at the range. We can see one of his rockets being launched'

So, we would go out into our backyard in our pyjamas and watch a rocket fly across the sky like a giant firework; it was so exciting as a kid.

When did music first speak to you?

Our parents would often take us to the biennial Adelaide Festival, and we'd stay with friends and attend performances. I remember hearing an orchestra for the first time at the age of six and just being overwhelmed by the spectacle of all those musicians and instruments that I was familiar with from listening to recordings but having never seen them played live before. So I knew about brass and wind, I knew about percussion and violins. But suddenly seeing the strings on stage, seeing the choreography of all the bows moving in the same direction, was magical. I remember as a six-year-old telling my mother that I really wanted to play the violin. But there was no school music programme in Woomera, so I had to wait until we moved to Adelaide in my later primary school years.

What made you take up the Viola?

I started with the violin, which was the only instrument small enough available at the school I went to when we came back to Adelaide, for someone who has always been challenged in the height department. My brother played viola and subsequently my younger sister played the cello, so we had a string trio at home. I was desperate to play in a primary schools' orchestra which contributed to a combined schools' music festival every year. Very quickly, I went from group lessons to individual lessons, and it was obvious that I had a musical ear. I've always been disciplined and practised regularly. I didn't mind practising, so I quickly made reasonably good progress.

You could audition for a single study position at the Conservatorium in Adelaide, so at High School, from the age of thirteen, I started lessons with Beryl Kimber. I really liked her and worked hard for her and made steady progress. I undertook AMEB exams, played in Eisteddfods and joined various Conservatorium Youth Orchestras and went to Music Camps. I reached AMEB grade seven in violin which was the top grade back then.

In the latter years of high school, when I was becoming more interested in other academic subjects, my enthusiasm for music persisted but my dedication to the violin started to wane. My teacher Beryl picked this up, which was indicative of her attentive teaching style. I had many musical friends a bit older than me who'd gone on to study music. Several were playing in rank-and-file positions in the Adelaide Symphony Orchestra. I noticed that they'd lost their passion for music. They didn't want to play chamber music anymore. And so suddenly, from only wanting to do music as a profession, I really didn't want to do that anymore.

That's how I changed to viola. Beryl saw that I wasn't as dedicated anymore and said, 'If you want to stay playing regularly, and I can see that you really enjoy your music, why don't you change to Viola because everybody always needs viola players. She also made the comment, which I don't agree with; "Technically, you can get away with less on the Viola." I think what she was really saying was you don't play right up on your E string in the stratosphere like violinists. I think the physicality of the viola demands greater strength and both left and right-hand technique than the violin

What was your most exciting musical experience as a player and then as a listener?

I've had some amazing ones, particularly being a musician in Darwin where I have lived for many years, including flying into Uluru to play. If you were a principal of a string section in the Darwin Symphony Orchestra (DSO), you automatically belonged to the DSO quartet. Jetstar commenced flights directly from Sydney to Uluru for the first time. We were asked to play at this dinner with all the Jetstar executives and many politicians. Our quartet was flown to Uluru for the occasion with the presence of the Rock looming as we played.

As a listener, my almost most vivid musical memory occurred when I was a child of about eight attending a concert with Benjamin Britten conducting the Adelaide Symphony Orchestra with his partner, Peter Pears, tenor, as the soloist. I didn't know about gay men and gay relationships, but I could see and feel the electricity of their connection. My mum and I were sitting really close to the front and I felt acknowledged both by the soloist and then the conductor. I think they sensed that as a child I was transported by their music-making and not in the least distracted.

I remember that electric feeling, perhaps because I'd grown up around my mother accompanying many singers, so I recognised accurate intonation, intimate musical partnership and their passionate musicality. I knew that something special was happening. There was an enormous bond between the two of them as they were performing. The piece was Britten's Serenade for tenor, horn, and strings. I had heard Britten's music before, as my parents listened to his operas including Peter Grimes, Billy Budd, Turn of the Screw etc.

What does music mean to you?

Music to me represents a part of my brain that is reliably calming, no matter what is happening in my life. It really anchors and grounds me. I get up in the morning and I put music on to have a shower to, I listen to music when I'm doing boring domestic chores, and when I write lengthy medico-legal reports. I listen to rock and roll at the gym and jazz when I cook. When I am reading, I listen to a different répertoire. Music calms me, it excites me, it switches me on in the morning and helps me to switch off at night. When I am playing or practising, and even before I knew what mindfulness and meditation were, I now know that's been what I experience through music.

As a Psychiatrist I've learned about the brain, where and how you listen, the link between those primitive parts of our brains, like with bird song and speech, the role of singing, of communication, and the impact of music on emotions. In dementia, and after strokes people who stop talking can still sing. People who stutter don't stutter when they are singing. Music has always been there for me. I'm sure in utero I heard a lot of Wagner. At Mt Buller one year, Edwina Kayser, the violinist, said to me 'My parents loved Wagner and I needed years of therapy to get through that.' I replied, 'And my parents loved Wagner, so I needed to become a psychiatrist to get over it.'

Can you remember when things went wrong in a performance?

It's funny as a listener, if things go wrong, it engages the audience more, especially once the performance comes back together. I think generally I get more out of a "flawed" compared with a flawless performance. You're listening to a quartet, and somebody forgets to repeat a section, the players just look at each other and often laugh. Then, someone might make a comment and then the performers start over. The whole audience is with them. Some of the mistakes I've heard have led to a heightened and more connected performance for both audience and performers.

In orchestras, as an experienced listener, I will hear, say, an early horn entry and as a musician, it will make me anxious. Then I see the conductor bringing the players back in. And phew, there is relief when it all comes back together. Yet to someone else who was there at the concert I'd say, 'oh God, the horns were lucky to pull that one off'. And my companion say, 'What are you talking about?' It's interesting that they thought the performance was flawless.

As a performer I don't think I have ever performed without making a mistake and obviously the critic in me, the imposter, only focuses on the mistake. But when as a doctor, we are trained that mistakes can be the difference between life and death, sometimes it is hard in my hobby to apply a lower standard to my performance.

What are your desert island choices?

Bach! I don't have to go much beyond Bach. If I'm sad Bach, if I'm happy, Bach, if I'm stressed Bach. If I'm angry I play Bach, which really soothes the Savage Beast, you know.

There would also be chamber music rather than the heavy symphonic repertoire. I love the voices and the intimacy of chamber music. Surprisingly, I don't listen to a lot of solo viola music because I prefer to hear the viola in an ensemble setting. I think the beauty of chamber music is that the whole is so much greater than the sum of its parts. When I hear a solo viola in film music, and I'm sorting out whether I'm listening to a cello high up, then suddenly realise it's the viola I'll find that 'aha' moment of how right the viola feels, especially in moments of melancholy.

How much do you practise?

It varies. During busy periods of my life, I literally put the instrument away. It stops being enjoyable because it starts becoming a burden and I haven't got the mental space to devote to it. Certainly, when there are upcoming concerts or Mt Buller Chamber School, I want to be able to play well. I want to be "Buller Fit" and be able to play and play for hours. The past few years, with Covid-19 restrictions, I've really missed Buller because I haven't had the stimulus to try to work up to an hour or two of regular practice. Normally I would only practice for an hour maximum because my head's 'done' after that, but preparing for the marathon of Buller pushes me beyond my usual pace and duration of playing.

When I'm working on something, I'd try and practise five days a week, for one hour. I've never been one to be able to do just 10 minutes of good practice a day, even though many teachers say it doesn't really matter how long you practise as just 10 minutes of daily focused practice can be enough.

Who were the most significant musical people in your life?

Beryl Kimber is a big one and in a way, Clemens Leskie (Sr) her husband. Listening to them play the violin and piano sonata repertoire as a teenager was so memorable and inspiring. Beryl was a fabulous violinist having gone to Russia and studied with David Oistrakh. In recent years, my musical connections are largely through ADO and Corpus Medicorum. People like Jean McMullin, Cath Brennan, Barb Manovel, Mary Muirhead, Sarah McGuiness, Richard Kueneman and Bronwyn Francis.

I remember attending an ADO chamber music day in Adelaide and lamenting that I would love to go to Buller, but knowing you had to go with a formed group. I couldn't do that from Darwin because at Christmas time there's an exodus as we all have interstate family obligations. I was talking to Bron and the others about how I would love to go to Buller. Then out of the blue the violist in their quartet pulled out and they asked me to join them. I don't think I have missed a year since except when I broke my wrist hiking.

What has ADO meant to you through the years?

When I very first played with ADO, I couldn't believe that the sound generated came from people who were all doctors as well as musicians. I found that absolutely amazing. We could play like an orchestra, having only just got together and our absolute heart and souls were in it. The very first concert I played if I correctly recall Keith Crellin conducted, and it was amazing just how he 'gets us'. It was such a beautiful marriage of a conductor that understood these bright, organised obsessional, dedicated people, all with little time but lots of passion and commitment and he knew how to rehearse us efficiently.

I also really enjoy playing with Corpus Medicorum. I mainly go down to Melbourne to play with Corpus now, as it's a minimum of five days with travel for ADO or Corpus and therefore it's really a week away from my family. I've found my orchestra niche with my colleagues in Corpus, and really, I couldn't do both easily so have had to prioritise.

Is there anything you want to ask me before we wind up?

Yes, I want to thank you, Miki. I think that without you, none of this, ADO or Corpus Medicorum, or any of the University Medical Orchestras which are all clearly modelled on ADO, would exist. Think the next musical medical generation will acknowledge what amazing foresight Dr Miki Pohl had. When you started this project, Australia would not have been as culturally aware, we weren't travelling overseas as a nation when you were agitating for something like this. And even interstate travel wouldn't have been that easy. Your capacity to connect disparate people with a common passion who are busy and bring them together to make music and perform together after so few rehearsals.

And so, Miki, I believe your vision, your commitment and your passion for the ADO have spawned so many progenies. I understand that there are doctors' orchestras in every state and territory as well as medical students' orchestras at so many universities. That is so good for all of us as pressured professionals to have such an important creative outlet. It has been your vision, your creativity, your generosity, and your passion for ADO which have allowed it to continue and that has been life-changing for so many of us.

And a question for you Miki: Did you think when you first started to connect people, did you ever imagine that it would be as successful and as widespread as medical orchestras have become?

Miki Pohl:

No, not at all, but I'll tell you it was a very anxious moment. That very first concert in '93, till we all got together, I had no idea what the standard would be. Yeah. Until I heard the first note, the first sort of sound, and I thought we're gonna be okay. You know, it was such a relief. Oh, immense relief. And it was a really good moment with Chris (Martin), conducting in the Melbourne Conservatorium of Music. We performed Mozart's The Abduction from the Seraglio overture. And we played Beethoven's third piano concerto with Bill Kimber, and a Haydn symphony.

Listen to This

COMPOSER	WORK	DETAILS	
Bach JS	St Matthew Passion	BWV 244	John Elliot Gardener
Bach JS	Solo Cello Suites	BWV 1007-1012	Ophélie Gaillard, János Starker, Gautier Capuçon,
Bach JS	Brandenburg Concertos	BWV 1046–1051	Early Music Ensemble (YouTube)
Bach JS	Chaconne	Partita no. 2 BWV 1004	Solo Violin Perlman, Milstein, Kremer
Barber	Adagio for Strings	From his String Quartet	Vienna Philharmonic / Dudamel (YouTube)
Bartok	Violin Duets	44 Duos / Sz 98	Végh Lysy recording
Beethoven	String Quartet Op.132	String Quartet No.15 Végh String Quartet	famous slow movement in the Lydian mode
Beethoven	Symphony No. 7	Op. 92	George Szell / Karajan
Beethoven	Triple Concerto	Op. 56	Agerich Piano / Capuçon brothers vln and Cello
Beethoven	Symphony No. 9	Op 125 "The Choral"	Famous "Ode to Joy"

COMPOSER	WORK	DETAILS	
Beethoven	String Quartets (16)	Early, Op. 18 (6) Middle, Op. 59 (3) Op. 74 & Op. 95 Late, Op. 127, 130, 131, 132, 133- (Grosse Fuge), 135	Végh String Quartet
Beethoven	Missa Solemnis	Op. 123	Shaw on Telarc / Bernstein NYP
Beethoven	Piano Concerto No. 5	Op. 73 "The Emperor"	Brendel / Rattle / Wiener Philharmoniker
Brahms	Symphony No. 1	Op. 68	Jansons / Vienna Philharmonic (2005)
Brahms	Piano Trios	Op. 8, 87, 101	Suk, Katchen, Starker
Brahms	String Sextets	Op. 18, Op. 36	Raphael Enseble
Brahms	String Quartet in C Minor	Op. 51	Belcea SQ
Britten	Cello Suites	Op.72,80,87	Rostropovich/ Mørk
Byrd	Mass for 4 & 5 Voices		King's Singers / The Tallis Scholars
Canteloube	Songs of the Auvergne	Kiri Te Kanawa	Decca No: 4449952
Chopin	Etude op 25		Baremboin
Debussy	L'après-midi d'un faune	L 86	Frankfurt Radio Symphony Andrés Orozco-Estrada
Don Burrows	Flute, Clarinet, Saxophone	A Tribute to Benny Goodman	many other YouTube clips

COMPOSER	WORK	DETAILS	
Dvorak	Cello concerto	Op. 104, B.191	Gautier Capuçon
Dvorak	Symphony No. 5	Op.76	Kubelik /Berliner Philharmoniker / DGG
Dvorak	Symphony No. 8	Op.88	Kubelik /Berliner Philharmoniker / DGG
Dvorak	Symphony No. 9	Op.95	Kubelik /Berliner Philharmoniker / DGG
Dvorak	Symphony No. 7	Op.70	Kubelik /Berliner Philharmoniker / DGG
Dvorak	"The American"String Quartet	SQ No.12 / Op.96	Hagen Quartet / DGG
Elgar	Cello Conerto	Op. 104	Du Pré / Fournier / Capuçon
Elgar	Enigma Variations	Op. 36	BBC SO/ Bernstein / DGG
Elgar	In the South	Op. 50	CBSO / Rattle/ Gramophone
Fauré	Piano Quartet	Op.15	Kungsnacka / Naxos
Fauré	Cantique de Jean Racine	Op.11	OAE / Kings College Cambridge / Cleobury YouTube
Franck	Violin Sonata		Oistrakh / Oborin
Franck	Symphony in D		New York Philharmonic / Kurt Mazur

Listen to This

COMPOSER	WORK	DETAILS	
Gibbons	The Silver Swan (1612)	Sung by	The Gesualdo Six
Glazonov	Violin Concerto	Op.82	Milstein / Fruhbeck de Burgos conducting
Goldmark	Violin Concerto		Philharmonia Milstein / Blech
Grieg	Piano Concerto	Op. 16	Buniatishvili / Sokolov
Gunaud	Faust	Opera premiered 1862	ENO / Plasson
Haydn	String Quartet	Op. 20 No. 5	Takács String Quartet
Haydn	String Quartet	Op. 76 No 5	Takács String Quartet
Holst	The Planets	Op. 32	Montreal / Dutoit
Hyde	Flute Sonatas		Aulos Australis
Khachaturian	Violin Concerto		Julia Fischer / RNO Kreisberg / Pentatone
Lalo	Symphonic Espagnole	Joshua Bell, Violin	Montreal Symphony Dutoit (Conductor) Decca
Mahler	Symphony No. 1	DVD Michael Tilson Thomas conducting	San Francisco Symphony Orchestra
Mahler	Symphony No. 2	Jurovsky conducting	London Philharmonic Orchestra
Mahler	Symphony No. 4	Iván Fischer conducting	Budapest Festival Orchestra / Channel Classics

Music Is Medicine

COMPOSER	WORK	DETAILS	
Mahler	Symphony No.5	Leonard Bernstein	Wiener Philharmoniker / DGG
Mendelssohn	Violin Concerto	Op.64	Menuhin or Milstein
Mendelssohn	Elijah / Oratorio	Op. 70	Fleming/ Terfel OAE / Decca
Monteverdi	Vespers 1610	Kings Consort	Robert King / Hyperion
Mozart	Viola Quintet C Major	K 515	Grumiaux Trio / Oxymoron I know!/ Phillips / Decca
Mozart	Horn Concerto	K 412, 417, 447, 495	Tuckwell / LSO / Maag
Mozart	Ave Verum Corpus	K618	The Sixteen / Harry Christophers
Mozart	Piano Concertos / Boxed Set	Mitsuko Uchida / Piano	English Chamber Orchestra Jeffrey Tate (Conductor)
Mozart	Clarinet Concerto	Wolfgang Meyer / Clarinet	Concentus Musicus Wien / Nikolaus Harnoncourt
Orff	Carmina Burana	YouTube - Live	Latin American YO and Chorus / Dudamel
Pärt Ärvo	Cantus	In Memory of Benjamin Britten	Proms-Albert Hall- Pärvi
Piazzola	Libertango	YouTube	12 Cellists of the Berlin Philharmonic

Listen to This

COMPOSER	WORK	DETAILS	
Prokofiev	String Quartets	Op 50 and Op 92	The American String Quartet
Rachmaninov	Symphonic Dances	Op. 45	Paavo Järvi / Orch Paris
Rafael Mendez	Trumpet	YouTube selection	
Ravel	Piano Concerto	in G Major	Grimaud / Jurovski
Rimsky-Korsakov	Scherezade	Op. 35	VPO/ Gergiev/2005 Salzburg Festival / YouTube
Saint-Saens	Carnival of the Animals	Capuçon chamber version on Virgin Classics also fabulous	Bergen Philharmonic / Neeme Järvi
Saint-Saens	Organ Symphony	Symphony No. 3	Charles Munch / Boston Symphony
Schostakovich	Piano Quintet	DVD Verbier Festival / 2008 MINDBLOWING!!	Agerich, Bell, Maisky, Beshmet, Henning
Schumann	Piano Quintet	Op.44	Kodály Quartet/ Jenö Jando Pno.
Schütz	Canticum Simeonis,	Funeral Music for Heinrich II of Reuss	The Marian Consort
Sculthorpe	Kakadu	SCM Symphony Orchestra	Barton (Didgeridoo)/ Diazmuñoz (Conductor)
Shostakovich	Symphonies 5,7,10,15	Best Boxed set of all the symphonies is with Haitink and the LPO and Concertgebouw	

Music Is Medicine

COMPOSER	WORK	DETAILS	
Shubert	Rosamunde String Quartet.	String Quartet No. 13 "Rosamunde"	Takács String Quartet (Decca)
Shubert	String Quintet	C Maj.	Orpheus String Quartet / Wispelwey (Cello)
Sibelius	Symphony No.2	Royal Concertgebouw Orchestra	George Szell / Conductor
Strauss Richard	Four Last Songs	Jessye Norman / Mezzo Soprano	
Strauss Richard	Alpine Symphony	Nelsons / BPO on their digital concert-hall! AWSOME!!!!!	CD / Kord / Warsaw Philharmonic
Strauss Richard	Horn Concerto	No 1 /Radovan Vlatkovic (Horn)	Radio Filharmonisch Orkest Stéphane Denève Conductor
Strauss Richard	Also, Sprach Zarathustra	CBSO / Orfeo label	Andris Nelsons (Conductor)
Stravinsky	The Rite of Spring	Otmar Suitner / Staatskapelle Dresden	Full Moon Classics
Stravinsky	Firebird Suite	Vienna Philharmonic Orchestra / (Decca)	Dohnányi 9Conductor0
Tallis	The Best of Thomas Tallis	Tallis Scholars / YouTube	Jeremy Summerly Conductor
Tchaikovsky	Souvenir de Florence	String Sextet / YouTube	Janine Jansen & Friends
Tchaikovsky	String Quartets	Kopelman String Quartet	Wigmore Hall Live (Label)

Listen to This

COMPOSER	WORK	DETAILS	
Vaughan Williams	The Lark Ascending	Nigel Kennedy	CBSO/ Rattle
Vaughan Williams	London Symphony Orchestra	Tallis Fantasia (LSO Label)	Antonio Pappano (Conductor)
Urbie Green	Trombone	JCV Jazz Festival	YouTube
Don Burrows	Flute Clarinet Saxiphone	A Tribute to Benny Goodman	many other YouTube clips

ADO Past Presidents

Miklós (Miki) Pohl *Cathy Fraser* *Mike Eaton*
1993-2003 *2004-2007* *2008-2010*

Rowan Thomas *Michaela Mee*
2011-2013 *2014-2016*

Anna Glue *Xavier Yu*
2017-2022 *2023-Currently*

Ackowledgements

Huge thanks to Hazel Edwards, not only for her excellent advice but also her continued and unwavering encouragement. I am also indebted to Dr Juliet Flesch who played a large role proofreading as well as Deidre Outhred. Suggestions were also gratefully received from Christene McGee in Hong Kong and Mary Clark Melbourne.

Leanne Dwight, my colleague, secretary and friend had an enormous part in typing, copying, printing proofs and formatting the manuscript.

Thanks also due to Ian Goding, Charles Ovadia, Chris Brown, Rick Reiner, Ted Arnold, Joe Canalese, Walter D'Onofrio, Gavin Frost, Ian MacDonald, Moya O'Shea in London, Haydn Perndt, Merrilee Robb and Michael Rozen, Barbara and Peter Kolliner, Bridget Byrne, Norman and Sandra Green in London for their suggestions.

Thanks also go to photographers Charles Frewen, Murray Stapleton and Greg Wallace.

Big thank you to Sylvie Blair and her team at Bookpod Publishing for their excellent advice and help through the publishing journey.

Thanks to my best friend Zoltán Kerestes for writing the back page blurb and offering his advice throughout.

A very special thanks to artist Tom Samek for the front and back cover and numerous other drawings throughout the book. Sadly, Tom passed away in 2021 in his early seventies from Motor Neurone Disease, hence all proceeds from sales are being passed on to Motor Neurone Disease, Victoria.

Providing and promoting the best possible care and support to people living with MND since 1981.

Please consider making a tax-deductable donation to MND Victoria.

www.mnd.org.au/music-is-medicine

MND Victoria is grateful to receive all profits from the sale of *Music Is Medicine* by Dr. Miklós Pohl OAM

www.ingramcontent.com/pod-product-compliance
Lightning Source LLC
Chambersburg PA
CBHW072151070526
44585CB00015B/1089